Unfurled

01 02 03 04 05 15 14 13 12 10

Caitlin Press Inc.
8100 Alderwood Road,
Halfmoon Bay, BC V0N 1Y1
www.caitlin-press.com

Text and cover design by Vici Johnstone and Pamela Cambiazo.
Edited by Debbie Keahey.
Printed in Canada on recycled paper.

Caitlin Press Inc. acknowledges financial support from the Government of Canada through the Canada Book Fund, the Canada Council for the Arts, and from the Province of British Columbia through the British Columbia Arts Council and the Book Publisher's Tax Credit.

Canada Council
for the Arts

Conseil des Arts
du Canada

BRITISH COLUMBIA
ARTS COUNCIL
We acknowledge the support of the Province of British Columbia through the British Columbia Arts Council

Library and Archives Canada Cataloguing in Publication

Unfurled : collected poetry from Northern BC women / [edited by] Debbie Keahey.

Poems.

ISBN 978-1-894759-52-6

1. Canadian poetry (English)—Women authors. 2. Canadian poetry (English)—British Columbian, Northern. 3. Canadian poetry (English)—21st century. I. Keahey, Debbie, 1961-

PS8283.W6U54 2010   C811'.60809287   C2010-904458-4

Unfurled

Collected Poetry from Northern BC Women

EDITED BY DEBBIE KEAHEY

CAITLIN PRESS

Contents

Acknowledgements   11

Preface   13

Jacqueline Baldwin   16

   16   Walking Toward the Main Doors
   18   I'll Leave the Fish Up High Where the Cat Can't Get at Them
   20   Heading East into the Rockies
   22   Wernicke-Korsakoff Lament
   23   'Tis You, 'Tis You
   24   Debriefing Session
   25   Wishing You Bread, Wishing You Roses

Leslie Barnwell   26

   26   I stand in the shower
   27   considering the possibility
   28   sign writer

Marilyn Belak   29

   29   Bissette Wetland
   30   Shearerdale Suite
   32   Flight Song
   33   The Fishing Poem

Katherine Bell   36

   36   Fragments
   37   Aggregate

Leanne Boschman   38

   38   Taken
   39   Sunday Lunch
   40   The Human Scent
   41   Prescription
   42   Terrace Revisited
   43   Northern Iconography
   44   spruce lullaby

Crystal Campbell   45

   45   past early
   46   The Burning
   49   whales

Joan Conway 50

50 Open for Business
52 Snapshots of Port Edward Cannery
54 Leaving Home

Barbara Coupé 55

55 The Ladies Dance
57 Red Clouds Dancing
59 Dormancy
60 The Question Marks of Ferns

Marita Dachsel 61

61 Main & Broadway
62 Presendia Huntington Buell
63 Agnes Coolbrith Smith
64 Fanny Alger
65 Marinda Johnson Hyde
66 Martha McBride Knight

Sarah de Leeuw 67

67 Travelling Three Lines

Pamela den Ouden 71

71 Preemie
73 Why I Don't Watch Movies
74 When Famous People Die
75 Doctor's Orders
76 Forecast
77 The Language of Trees

fyre jean graveline 78

78 Oh Canada. Our Canada. One of Four Against.
85 White Noise

Jamella Hagen 86

86 An Introduction to My Mother
88 My Father Explains
89 After the Moon's Gone Down
91 Field Mice
92 Leaving the North

Lisa Haslett 93

93 Carving Out

94 The Distance Between Trees
96 Fat Free
97 François Lake. Autumn, 1992.

Jacqueline Hoekstra 98

98 Skeena floods again
100 Fishing with my father
102 Old Growth
103 At Lakelse Lake I forget you again

K. Darcy Ingram 104

104 So many years later
107 Small bones
109 In Montana
110 Interiors

Donna Kane 111

111 Visitation
112 Resonant Frequency
113 In the Middle of Dinner
114 Epiphenomenalism
115 Fungus Love
116 Bee

Sabrina L'Heureux 117

117 Car nap
119 What I'm left with
120 Weighing poetry
121 Dance Partner
122 Ode to tea drinkers

Caroline Lowther 124

124 Alterations

Mary MacDonald 126

126 Paddling Bowron Lakes
129 The journey that you are

Pua Medeiros 131

131 Skun Gwaii
133 The Object
135 This Morning I Complained
137 With Your Silver Spoon Shoved Firmly Up Your Ass
139 Coyote and the Anthropologist

Sheila Peters   141

141 The Buttercup Poems

Rebekah Rempel   146

146 Cowbirds
147 Frogs
148 I Breathed Deeper, Trying
149 How to Honour the Dead
150 My Mother's Hands

Laisha Rosnau   151

151 A New Kind of Fire
152 Bolt
153 Hard Won
154 Play Off Season
155 Frame

Joanna Smythe   156

156 translations of the rain
158 this northern lake
159 arctophobia

Carly Stewart   160

160 deterring our minds some
162 full shot to skeletons

Si Transken   163

163 Sunday Shift
165 Distinguish This
167 Bullies with Designer Lipstick
169 Purple
170 Casual Pleasures of Aging Well
171 Protest Prep 101
172 Dancing at Another Feminist Party

Patricia June Vickers   173

173 Peradventure
175 Swanaskxw
176 Northwesterly Naxnox
177 She bends
178 Separation

Denielle Wiebe 179

179 when we are twenty-four again tomorrow
180 under the philosophers' stones
181 wet siren
182 nursery rhyme
183 a simple trout

Gillian Wigmore 184

184 gaps in the downtown revitalization efforts, september two thousand eight
185 Pine: a love story
189 bather at a spring
190 Debbie: two things:
193 spring

Alice Williams 194

194 Intemperate Rainforest
195 Tom
196 Waiting for the Float Plane
197 Poetry

Contributors 199

About the Cover 207

207 Absolute Depth by Jacqueline Rush Lee

Acknowledgements

My deep appreciation goes to Rob Budde — partner, poet and Prince George cultural ambassador — who first saw the need for this collection and then assisted in ways too numerous to mention to help bring it to fruition.

I'm grateful also to Gillian Wigmore and Laisha Rosnau, who each at various points stepped up to help bump the project along to the next stage. I think it has turned out better than any of us could have imagined, and hope you will be proud to have had a hand in it early on.

Huge thanks to all the writers who contributed their work, often working intensively with me to ensure each piece achieved its full potential, and responding quickly and with good humour to my many "urgent" requests along the way. It was a great pleasure and privilege to get to know you all and to assist in bringing your work to publication.

Thanks also to the women who submitted work that I was unable to use this time around. I hope you'll keep working on your writing and submitting to other venues.

For assisting with the financial and psychological space that allowed me to devote myself to this project, thanks to the University of Northern British Columbia English Program and my four children: Robin who recognized my wild-eyed look and took on extra responsibilities so I could focus, Erin who kept the "littlers" entertained, Quin for many days giving up his beloved "computer time" so I could use the machine, and Anya for joyfully starting preschool at just the right time for both of us. Finally, thanks to Vici Johnstone of Caitlin Press for her vision and commitment to supporting Northern BC and women's literature.

Some of the poems in this collection previously appeared, often in different form, in the journals and magazines *Malahat Review, Room, Island Writer Magazine, Event, Fiddlehead, Arc Poetry Magazine, dANDelion, Critical Social Work Journal* and the *Antigonish Review*, in chapbooks or online in Leaf Press's "Monday's Poem."

Preface

Debbie Keahey
Prince George
June 22, 2010

This collection has often seemed to be a long time coming, but it actually developed quite quickly as things go in the publishing world. It had its origins in a discussion a couple of years back between Rob Budde, my partner and a professor of creative writing at the University of Northern British Columbia, and Ottawa poet Rob McLennan, in an interview published in the *Danforth Review*. Talking about the dominant view of the Prince George writing scene and Northern culture in general as being overwhelmingly male territory, Budde expressed his concern about how this view — whether perception or reality — might disadvantage women writers in the area. Being a long-time community-builder and supporter of local culture, a political aesthetic we share and brought to Prince George from our years living in Winnipeg, Budde had the idea of putting together a collection of Northern BC women's writing.

Gillian Wigmore and I, who had been enjoying weekly coffee and kid play-dates, eagerly took up the project and quickly secured Caitlin Press's interest in publishing it. Vici Johnstone had recently taken over the press and was reinvigorating it with her special interests in Northern writers and women's writing. Enthusiasm ran high in all quarters, but the looming and largely unspoken question was: would we really be able to get enough good writing to fill a whole book? This seems almost funny in retrospect, since it turned out there was enough excellent writing to do a book just of poetry (a companion volume or two of short prose and creative non-fiction is in the works), but the question reflected how little any of us knew about who was "out there" writing.

In her poem *Debbie: two things:*, included in this volume, Gillian asks "where are the women writing in PG?" I had been very active in the Winnipeg writing community, but when Rob and I moved to Prince George in 2001 the combined pressures of having babies #3 and #4, teaching online university English courses, building two different home-based businesses, supporting his career and living in a semi-rural area outside of town, meant I all but disappeared from public view. There was no time, brain-space or incentive for writing. While the image of the poet working away for years or a lifetime in unrecognized isolation is a popular romantic myth, the reality is that writers, like other humans, are primarily social beings, and poetry, like other forms of writing, is as much about readers as it is about writers.

Women typically lead doubly-busy lives, and this combined with the distances and geographical isolation of life in the North may help explain why, apart from small pockets of mentorship and support, there has not been much sense of community or tradition for women writing in this region to draw on. Problems of busyness and distance also slowed work on this project, as Gillian had to step down as co-editor to take on a full-time job and Laisha Rosnau, who took on the role, soon had a new baby and then moved away due to her husband's work. Finally, I ended up sole editor, and the book editing process reflected the very reasons it was such a necessary project.

My goal, moving forward, was to assemble as large and diverse a group of writers as possible, with writing quality being the overriding selection criteria. In terms of experience, some of the writers gathered here have published one or more books, while some have published in journals or chapbooks, and for others this is their first publication. Some have received national attention and awards, some are well-known in the North or throughout BC, and some are unknown outside their immediate circle of acquaintances. Many of the writers gathered here have experienced a sense of creative community while honing their craft in creative writing programs at UNBC, UBC, UVIC, and elsewhere. A few others have been fortunate enough to create or find small networks of writing support in their immediate communities. Many have experienced an absence of regular readership and critical feedback that they feel has hampered their development, a gap which I hope this book will begin to rectify.

The pleasures of the reader have been utmost in my mind as I put this collection together, and the poems run the gamut from lyric, imagist, narrative, oral and experimental styles. There are poems about family, food, death, political activism, love, coffee, and lots and lots of nature, as might be expected in an area where human settlements comprise such a small portion of the physical and psychological space. Where my own bias shows most is in my preference for work that shows attention to form, that is true to its own style and voice, and that demonstrates precision of image and language. The poetry here is by turns tough, sensitive, sensuous, provocative, funny, moving, wise, accessible, challenging and entertaining, and the collection can be dipped into randomly or read straight through with equally rewarding results.

My overall hope for this book is that it clearly announces (both to ourselves and the "outside world") the presence of a diverse, vibrant and skilled community of Northern BC women poets, that it connects writers with writers, writers with readers, and readers with readers. Let the celebrations begin.

Jacqueline Baldwin
Prince George

Walking Toward the Main Doors

spring is late this year
much thawing and bitter refreezing has left
lumps and bumps and slippery
glassy frozen puddles to navigate
from the far end of the high school parking lot

I tread carefully in elegant but impractical shoes
reach safety beneath the roof overhang with great relief
then, early for an appointment as a classroom guest
walk slowly along the ice-free concrete pathway
that skirts the brick-walled gymnasium

on the right-hand side of the path
where snow has melted and refrozen time after time
a long line of thick ice has formed
trapping within it the detritus of what
others have lost, discarded
as they sought shelter here

narratives held captive in ice
someone's hockey tuque frozen where it fell
a few condoms
one perfect golden maple leaf
one very small forlorn woolen glove
two crumbled chocolate chip cookies embalmed
in their cellophane package

a black banana peel lies in
four gracefully joined semicircles of
ice-bound calligraphy

near the door lies a yellow package of
zig-zag rolling papers
its cover torn apart to reveal dozens of
pristine white rice-paper leaves
spread out in accordion precision

only one corner is imprisoned, held fast by the ice
the other three corners float free
the rice papers flutter back and forth in a beautiful dance
performing a miniature rectangular ballet
turning, turning, in unison with each breath of wind
like a flock of ecstatic birds
dipping and diving in flight

I'll Leave the Fish Up High Where the Cat Can't Get at Them

John brings me some rainbow trout
fresh from Purden Lake
tells me he thought I would still be out, over at the school

I give him a poem for his mother in Vancouver
she is seventy-nine, twenty years older than he is
we are lucky, he says, to have her still here

we stand in the sun talking about senses
how there are more than we ever knew
when we were younger
but nobody taught us how to engage them
and how sometimes, especially out on the water
you feel quite sure you have
been here before on this earth
a knowing so strong that wild horses
couldn't drag you away from the certainty of it

I have to go back to work I say
me too he says
I am planting carrots and beets today

I walk out to his pickup truck with him
me in my fancy dancy high-heeled city shoes
caramel leather
he in blue jeans and the
whitest T-shirt I have ever seen
whiter than white against his
curly black hair and tanned face

the pickup is loaded high with beautiful soil
from his friend's poultry farm in Pineview
I dig my hands into the aged richness of years old
pure black composted chicken manure
homesick for the feel of my own farm at Loos, between the
Cariboo Ranges and the Canadian Rockies

yup, he says, I am off home to the lake
got a load of chicken shit for my vegetable garden
I have fish in the lake
firewood split and piled by the cabin
what else do I need? he grins
I am a happy man

Heading East into the Rockies

John doesn't usually pick them up
what with the world being the way it is now
which means
almost indecipherable to him
even worse than it was when he was seventeen and
desperately searching for clues about how to be

besides, he hates the moment of
dropping them off at his turnoff
alone on a deserted highway
he worries about them for weeks afterward

now he is fifty-seven
driving the forty miles home to the lake he sees this
unkempt, pale kid, maybe nineteen, with his thumb out
just past the turnoff to the airport
carrying his stuff in
one black plastic garbage bag
so thin he looks concave
hunched into the wind from the
passing semis and logging trucks
heading East on Yellowhead Sixteen

John pulls over thinking:
what the hell am I doing

the hitchhiker jumps in
smiling like a child given a surprise treat
says he is going all the way to Edmonton
see if he can do any better there
Prince George wasn't such a good idea with
all the rain in the past week
nowhere to curl up and sleep

Molly the black lab sits silent between them
she is John's lifeline
his armour against what he
no longer understands

nice dog
says the hitchhiker
nice dog

I know, says John, she is my friend
my best friend ever, really
meaning it absolutely

the hitchhiker exclaims:
oh! oh! I have a friend too
I do, I do
he goes everywhere with me and
I love him
he is in here

with great excitement
he opens the black plastic bag
pulls out a tattered teddy bear
rubbed clean of all its fur
torn at the edges
handled so much it looks
bedraggled, long, empty, wrung out

the boy holds the teddy bear up in the air
gazes at it adoringly
his face aglow

see, I have a friend
I am so glad you have a friend
look, we *both* have a friend

he smiles in contentment
sitting on the passenger side of a
fifty-thousand dollar pickup truck
closely hugging what remains of the teddy bear
chanting the words over and over

so glad, so glad
I am so glad we both have a friend
so glad we both have a friend
so glad, so glad
so glad

Wernicke-Korsakoff Lament

Spanish neuroscientist and artist Santiago Ramón y Cajal won the Nobel Prize in 1906 for his work in discovering that neurons are separated from one another by narrow gaps. This is how in 1871 he described the structure of neurons: "The aristocrat among the structures of the body, with its giant arms stretched out like tentacles of an octopus to the provinces of the frontier side of the outside world, to watch for constant ambushes of physical and chemical forces."

it is now known that the effect of too much alcohol
on the brain
exacts a terrible price

I cannot watch this any longer
the constant presence of grief
destroys me

grieving for the living whose
spirit is no longer visible
despite physical presence
grieving even while love still lures with
songs of past joy

I hear the beloved voice
see the blue eyes, but cannot forget
there is turmoil within a mind where
neurotransmitters and
dendrites as beautiful as trees
jangle in distress as they
fail to connect to their destinations
but still valiantly, faithfully, desperately
reach out their arms

like swimmers
drowning
inches away from a life raft

'Tis You, 'Tis You

last night she dreamt he was a baby again
hair the colour of sun-bleached straw
his toddler body clinging to hers as they swim
laughing and together
from log to log on Stave Lake

in the swimming dream she holds the baby tight
enfolds him as she kicks along, backstroke
while he, chuckling with delight
hangs on for dear life to his mother's body
convinced it is he who maintains this
delicious motion in the water
his eyes dancing in a face that knows nothing but
love, trust, and the wonder of the moment

in the flickering shadows of the dream stands
someone else
an image of the same person as an adult
a tall, strong, gorgeous man thirty-five years old
still closely connected to his mother but
addicted
his eyes full with sorrow and pain after
a night spent in jail
for being drunk

in the dream background the grown man's image
begins to move slowly toward them
as if through thick fog
he rests his head wearily on one shoulder
says to the mother:

don't let him see me like this, please

Debriefing Session

her living room art studio is in disarray and
full of friends from anthropology class
talking about assignments due
daycare, women's lives, politics, children

someone has brought foccacia bread
a pot of green tea steams
on the bare wood of the oak dining table

this impromptu gathering develops into one of
profound discussion and connection that
makes her want to paint but
her new canvas is not yet cut, nor
stretched onto frames so she grabs a
folded brown paper grocery bag from her kitchen to
secure the image before it flies away, and
on the thick grainy paper
paints quickly in voluptuous purple brush strokes
a woman's back
tranquil in repose
head bent, the neck lit with
subtle streaks of sunshine yellow
the background vivid orange

not religious in the formal sense
she prays a lot
for peace, her children, her aging parents

she tells us she knows an Asian doctor who can
pray only, *only* when wearing a tuque
he is a man who says he just cannot pray
tuque-less
this makes her wonder if there is a Canadian god who
understands snow, is not vindictive
and does not dispense shame and guilt for free

someone still thinking about the Asian doctor
slowly murmurs:
Alice, B., Tuque-less
the room erupts in riotous laughter

Wishing You Bread, Wishing You Roses

this is for
you

for all the times you act honourably
even when nobody is looking
when you fearlessly fight injustice and ignorance
armed only with the passion of your own knowing

for the times you weep with frustration
about the lives of women
the depth of their pain
the weight of their burdens

this is for you
for walking with courage through danger
protecting the weak
nurturing the young
working
tired through to the bone
as if the world depended on you

which it does

you who are a
wise, strong, kind woman, a
humourous, sensitive, understanding woman, a
life-giving, life-sustaining, passionate woman, a
tenacious, outspoken woman,
an unafraid woman

you keep on singing and dancing in your soul
no matter how difficult the challenges
how mountainous the barriers
you value the spirit of the little girl you were
allow her to live, secure, within your grown self

I salute you
and join you on the road toward
a fine balance

bread on one side, roses on the other
both flourishing

Leslie Barnwell

The Kispiox Valley

I stand in the shower

its flow
washes me and I
do not resist the power
of memory
or of metaphor

water streams over my body
covers my face
when I close my eyes a wall of rock
rises behind me and water falls
upon me from the greatest height

my hands caress the roundness
of my belly and I remember for an instant
how it felt to be pregnant
how it felt to wait
for the inevitable, the impossible
at the same time
how it felt
to know you would break free
and would never break free

I balance this
moment before your birth
on the crest of time's wave

you were born after all
and water always remembers

considering the possibility

perhaps some people really do sleep
all night long and do not cry out
maybe their sheets are not snares
they move with long strides their arms
swing in rhythm
music pours from their mouths
long lines of quarter notes, halves,
undulating like rivers
birds eat them and the song rises

perhaps some of us are not afraid
and some, though not many, never fall
maybe blindness does not hinder them
they see truth as clearly as that butterfly
resting there on the branch its silver-spotted
underwings tilted to gather sunlight
they grasp it quickly before it darts away
maybe some of us actually get it right

sign writer

it is no easy task tacking memories on public billboards in the rain.
don't expect any assistance. i think i remember a time when it all stayed
put, when the colours didn't run and wind didn't grab at the edges and
tear. or maybe that was just a dream. out here in the garden with the
evening grosbeaks cutting yellow chunks out of the air it doesn't make
as much sense.

i will stay here until further notice. maybe the sodden message of my
signs will change, grow clearer as the inks run into each other. lighten.
there are so many words i have yet to speak, so many fragments of
poems going nowhere, loose language like so many feathers without
birds.

Marilyn Belak

Dawson Creek

Bissette Wetland

still, there are epiphanies:
in the wetland drought
you face twilight, its optical tricks

an aberrant wand of sun
casts its final lure to willow flycatcher,
riffs the mumble of ducks and sighs
into reed bed shadows

wake-song: a goose draws
its line past the moon
and slips into obsidian
pond, a ripple etched
in glassy night

Shearerdale Suite

Grouse

on the slope
coyote den spills
bones, a beak
eroded rhamphotheca, silent

the familiar grouse skeleton
furcula of wishes
from the hunt platter
drumsticks tossed near
sail-like synsacrum

the naked head speaks
life, its absence

Summer

in silver-grass and sage
you stretch above the sepia
slow Kiskatinaw and turning leaves

doubting there could
be more beauty, you let it
pass like the brief

sweep of an eagle
caught in the corner
of your vision
too fleeting for truth

Kiskatinaw River Ravens

1.
ravens play the river-sky
loop, tumble, switchback

2.
we ski under the bridge
and follow deer tracks
to the icicle and water dance
of a drink-hole bourée —
remember violin recitals
our young son's black-suited arm
graceful, fingers flying

3.
Sunday slides away
on snowmobile's wake
glide — pole — glide
attention tied to the sky
where raven pairs swing
slow — slow
quick — quick — ͝
     slow

Flight Song

the few long summer days
fly by with birds you neglect
to count and a lover
who witnesses the moon drop
drunk on blanket fields
tipping the night to its lips
and stags on their way to water

one upland sandpiper
flight-song fills the endless twilight
beyond silence, inky barbs
write a haiku on the wire
to the next post, where
she poses, wings akimbo

The Fishing Poem

what I wanted was
to write about catching the trophy fish

not about that long day

I spent on the shale bank beside the road
on the Tahltan River when my husband
and his father left at dawn
to fish on the reserve
when they didn't come back until after dark

when my son was one
and napped all day while I watched

Grizzlies cross the bar downstream

when there was nowhere to walk but away
from my sleeping child or towards the bears
and I knew no cars or trucks would come until the road crew
returned from Telegraph to Dease that night

when by noon all the chores were done   even supper
ready to go on the campfire and I bathed the baby in the dishpan

I didn't want to say
that the travelling songs we belted
on the way hadn't prepared me for this

or to wonder
how the plan to take his dad had changed
to taking a cook and her baby

I wanted to talk about
the icy water spinning under
the bridge — the silence of naked rock
and lichens — of solitude and wilderness

but the road turned away from my narrow
shoulder-camp on one side and curved over
the bridge on the other and sacred

Klabona lands stretched north forever
you see they took the truck and the gun
I can't remember
                how it got decided
only the dumb surprise when they left

        and that it's odd

how I got used to the Grizzlies crossing
                heard kingfishers and the *shshshsh* of shale
                when I climbed the bank to check the baby
                or watch the grey river water boil
                white around bridge pilings

how late in the afternoon I decided
                to spin cast a straight hook for trout
                caught an eight-pound Dolly and another
                and then a silver streak tore my line downstream
                spun through the air and dove for the bridge

how it was time to check my child
                and I didn't cut the line
                and half an hour later I told myself
                fifteen minutes and I would and later
                that if he cried I'd hear him

how after an hour the fight was maybe
                weaker and soon I would bring him in
                and every few minutes I thought the men
                or the crew would come

how when the rod snapped
                I wrapped the line over   and over
                my right hand and braced
                        my feet behind a boulder
                got sprayed when he rose so close
                to shore   he flew over my head
                onto the bank and I didn't have a club

how I stunned him with a rock
       clutched him to my breast — stumbled
       up the bank and threw him on the road
       the sound he made leaping on the gravel

       while I dug for my knife
       grabbed him on his way over the edge
       drove it into his spine
       and with him scooped
       in my arms we slid back to the river

       I washed him and washed myself in his water

but what I really wanted to tell was

that when the road crew stopped by
I was drinking wine by the fire
while the supper cooked the baby played
and those guys weighed and measured and recorded
the Dollies and the Steelhead and listened
to my story
before they got the whisky from their truck
toasted me and sat to wait for the fishermen

       that in the end
       my Steelhead was nineteen pounds
       to their best fourteen

that I wore the good dress I had packed
for Vancouver, and firelight
flashed gold from my waist-long hair

Katherine Bell

Lakelse

〜

Fragments

I am from smashed glass,
black eyes, and violent voices.
I am from gunpowder, pain,
and insecurity, the threat
of drunk ignition.

I am from valium and barren shelves,
I am from a mother who refused
to beg for money and a garage filled with
empty rum and coke bottles.

I am fragments — a glass ketchup bottle
slipping from a child's careless hands,
a father's blast shaking her bones.
I am from cold silences and scathing rages,
I am from the stillness that descended
when he returned from work.

I am from uneasy sleep and his fist slamming
the dining room table, the crippling of the
brass-topped stand and the wall clock
needing glue again.

I am from "take your children and get the fuck out,"
"please god, make him go away, please,"
and "you are just like your father," dirt

that never washes off.

Aggregate

I am from unwashed wool,
carders, spinning wheels, and looms.
I am from gunpowder, shells,
and freezers stuffed
with beaver pelts.

I am from scrabble, backgammon, mah-jong.
I am from women gathered
around our dining room table —
laughing, smoking, drinking thick coffee
and playing rummoli late at night
with pennies and tired eyes.

I am aggregate — sandcastle building
and jumping the waves.
I am from fresh crab and homemade root beer.
I am from snow angels,
snow caves and icicles three feet long.

I am from easter at grandma's: turkey and stuffing,
mashed potatoes with gravy, brussel sprouts
(fed to the dog under the table),
olives and pickles, yams and sweet potatoes,
grandpa's dandelion wine.

I am from "eat a little bit of everything,"
"if you are going to fight, go outside,"
"get an education first," and love,

unspoken.

Leanne Boschman

Prince Rupert

Taken

Dark insinuations of probes, ultrasound, x-rays — finally
the week arrives when my mother receives her test results.

Back home a few grey and rust-brown feathers on the deck.
Do birds fly unsuspecting into these windows? Can't help

wondering what that moment would be like: the glassy thud,
stunned with the future still in plain view,

but you are not headed in that direction any longer.
No way to tell for certain where any new trajectory leads.

Sitting up on the tree house platform in the afternoon,
I wonder if it's better to be like these dandelions leaning

on straw-thin stalks, no resemblance to their buttery —
bright former selves. They don't know

if the next breeze might be the one. White seeds flying,
taken by the wind.

Sunday Lunch

An acorn squash, a yam, two potatoes all split in half,
baked until flesh is soft, thin crust scraped away.

Gingery steam fills the kitchen as I search for ingredients;
soon, as usual, I'm improvising.

A hot orange spatter flies out of the soup pot;
my mother at the table, our kitchen talk urgent these days.

She always made my favourite soup, a summer borscht
whenever I came home — even in winter, managed to find

sorrel and savory. Before her chemotherapy began,
the doctors outlined the effects and her chances in exact terms

and percentages, not factoring in the fierce spirit
that remained as her body dwindled to this thinness

that has me checking the cupboards again, trying to guess
the perfect ingredient or morsel she could not resist.

Last of all, buttermilk, just sour enough to perform
the alchemy that results in praise for flavour and shade.

I watch anxiously to see how much she has eaten, urge
one more spoonful to counteract chemicals that scald,

all of us searching for the right recipes.

The Human Scent

Her hair is still in the red bag on a shelf in the spare room.
Guests don't know — I never say here are some towels,

an extra blanket if you get cold, and this is my mother's hair
beside the board games and paperback dictionary.

She gave it to me the day after it fell out, a few weeks after
her treatments began, a week after the deer had eaten

buds from the yellow rose bush planted in August,
only spindles of stems left and too late in the season for more.

It's the human scent that keeps deer away from plants
someone had told her, and she seemed happy, as if

this solved a predicament for both of us. So why can't I
scatter her hair in the garden?

I could save a few strands the way Victorians kept a beloved's
lock in a brooch, but perhaps this bag of hair is a charm

to ward off the day when only keepsakes remain,
and tracks left by hungry deer fill in with drifting snow.

Prescription

The doctor said time alone would ease
these winter ailments, now spring temperatures
unseasonably low.
But there was something more virulent slinking
through my capillaries, sticky thoughts,
chronic doubts, like coughing fits that left me weak.
More difficult each morning to leave
  the cave of sleep.

According to black birds, this condition isn't fatal.
The way crows soar their darkness,
                 then settle on the lightest boughs.
Ravens, their raucous songs, gurgling
up from the cross-flow of moans,
                    shrieks

of laughter.

A consultation at twilight, they prescribed the cure —
  chants accompanied by clinking of chimes
made of sea glass, rusty nails, and water
  sloshed in discarded calabashes.
Prayers to be intoned while thumbing
  a rosary of agates, marmot bones, and emeralds.

Now I savour each sip of cottonwood
sap that reaches me from the river's bed, each wave
of sunlight that crashes through the window
        knocking everything to the floor,
    while dark wings flap overhead.

Terrace Revisited

At the Saturday morning farmers' market these runty
northern apples will likely end up sauced
Cellophane-wrapped butter tarts, bread lined up on folding tables,
hand-knit socks dangle beneath tarps along with waist aprons,
broods of baby bonnets.
Bouquets from Portuguese flowerbeds that brim with red
dahlias, calico asters.

I'm a visitor now to this town, my home not so long ago
but long enough to notice new lines cross-hatched into faces
of women in this amiable living room — its pocked floor,
photos of teens in grad gowns.
In the drum circle my hands find each beat again, and I'm lulled
awhile by this midday rhythm; then after goodbyes
surprised by my urge to toss the gift of silver
dollar seeds to the wind and run down back alleys pitching apples.

Northern Iconography

On television news a boy with mesh-cap securing sutures,
and another who now calls the valiant dog his guardian.
The photo of the cougar startles most —
head surprisingly small against red-marbled snow,
paws curled back tenderly toward its chest,
an interrupted embrace.

The camera doesn't capture a child asleep, lamp left on,
and the other boy whose legs twitch beneath log cabin quilt.
Golden retriever convulsed — perhaps pinned once more,
stitches traced beneath disinfected fur.
The brave officer's pistol snug in its leather holster,
only his snores snipe into shadows.
A mother's shoulders adrift against a muslin ridge,
rows of tiny hairs still standing sentinel in her ears.

spruce lullaby

heaving swoop of such
 heavy boughs trailing fronds,
you are not a sleek tree
  slow swinging through my days.
sweep of your lapsed greenery
framed in the window where i need
to see you just outside the blue fence.
  droopy oldtree & at the same
time such a plush damntree,
  overgrown but i look at you
to know my cradle will be rocked.
  through swindling gusts & crush
of snow & rain splatter
 i will be rocked,
swishswung safely even if
  dangling over my stony times
even when my own momma passes
  from this earth & papa toooo
when they in alluvial rest & no more
  can i go back to talk our familiar talk
evening talk & mended clothes,
  even then i will be rocked.

i've been afraid that i will slump
  when it's time to be mighty, afraid
i will lower when it's time
  to tower when calamities that seem far
away shake the ground right below me.
  it might get harder to breathe
for me as cities fume i'll still need
  your musky exhalation, but mostly
tonight i need tonight i need to hear
              the lull-a-bye shush
                    of your darkgreen song.

Crystal Campbell

Prince George

past early

dark fibre plateau littered
with glass mugs and the tattered
remains of toast. corpse
grey sky and wrinkled
lines of worry mark time.

the cup, once drawn up,
encompasses noise in a crater
of silence. heat of day
steams from the rim, minds
the final drop.

warmth seeps into the seams
between muscle and tendon
defining the first sip, a syllable
marked by contraction.

The Burning

1.

On burning day, coffee breathed
acid and the alarm clock slowed its tick.
I was late for work.

Fire purifies, ridding us of the excess.
Smoke is an uneasy buy,
product of success. Twitching
fingers probe a half-empty purse.

Cigarettes are there,
somewhere.

2.

The first smoke curl came
through cedar shakes, unwilling
to stay in dark space. It danced
in sunlight, played hopscotch, gyrated
around an unseen pole. The nightclub
was a bad influence.

They had comedy, while others had
lobster tails or steak. Orders of laughs
in a half rack on special, the third
Friday of the month. The brat pack had
a following.

Keep under the eaves and wait for the door
to open and joy to butt out, with a second
puff and drag, bump
and grind. The trusses groan.

3.

Skeletons glow with fright after
a shot of tequila and energy. The worm
eats wood, makes trails like old
breaks in a femur challenged by age. Only
a few feet of wall stood after
the barrage. Bones last longest.

4.
It drips down, hot
from under the metal façade. Sweat
snakes down to pavement,
as fighters climb into the ring.

They try to box it in
but the cedar shakes
them off and entices bets
on the twelfth round odds.

Cops plank salmon on cedar
to serve it hot when the fire goes out.

5.
A strange entryway
to an old building. Long dark hall
and foyer into nowhere but a cubbyhole
office that smells of cooking oil.

Mediocre restaurant but
it had a grand piano and pretensions
to high society. Well-done
steak was rare, all dressed and
nowhere nice to go.

Walls of burnt oatmeal, where timber
fell and made noise. Someone
was there to hear it, chewing cheap
sandwiches from the Mr. G's,
and sipping *Evian* water.

6.
The only thing left was
the vault. Hundreds of boxes,
metal and concrete storage
for paper memories.
You fold them, make
cranes and snowflakes.
A thousand will get you one wish
that comes true. The manager

wishes she hadn't come to work.
No time to fold
keepsakes or remember
they were there.

Let the door crash and lock it,
leave with purse in hand, looking
for the package of death in the bottom.
Light up once you cross over.

Everything changes if there are
no fireguards.

whales

notes lie beached on stained
carpet crossed gaze of wisdom
shores itself against apathy
in an ocean of percentages

come up to air
above the surface tension
of journal and lecture recirculated

liquid pours into the mold
of a mind that holds its breath
and dives against the tides

breach above in the gulf
between salt and north star
pinpoint the longitude of reason
to give latitude and lecture

theory and hypothesis
sink into the specifics of plankton
an exhale of bubbles marks
slack logic in the free current
of academia

Joan Conway

Terrace

ᔕ

Open for Business

The house plunked square centre at the dead end of Kalum Street
appears as though it was always there. Always the stage
for slow moving CN trains chugging in its rear,
cars loaded with saw chips heading east.
The peaked roof bears a Union Jack flag,
flapping in the chill October afternoon.
It appears to be waving at the almost empty street,
at the fitted brick sidewalk winding
its way around a patch of turf
too green for this late in the fall.
Waving at the cedar tourism sign announcing
one of Terrace's early pioneers,
George Little, lived here.

His wife, Clara Beste Little, designed the house
but it is George who is quoted as saying
"You can't get ahead in life until you have a nest."

"Get ahead" rings off its grand entranceway,
off freshly painted white pillars surrounding the porch.
Thick timber doors polished in oil-finished gleam,
large wrought iron windows framed on either side.
"Get ahead" reflects off a paddlewheel model on display.
Boats that forge new frontiers
push along banks of the Skeena River,
torrents of water pounding their bodies.

Ahead in life, new life —
the sawmills spewing out logs and chips.
George Little, the first pioneer to start
a mill in this town, to hire its first employees.

The house tall and white
against blackened bodies of the CN rail line,
cars in motion rattle as they joust into position,
clang and groan under their weight.
Iron frames pick up speed, roll ahead
past the house, past neatly trimmed lawns,
empty park benches inviting rest.

Tall and white against
the only other building on this block,
the Terrace Hotel, equally anchored.
Its squat body lined with windows
reflecting the grey afternoon sky.

At the corner stands a man.
He doesn't look at the house.
His head tilts,
listening, watching.
Eyes blending into long thick hair,
into dark skin of crushed velvet
draped inside a black jacket
that flaps open in the breeze.
He does not look at the park benches.
Does not rest here.

The house tall and white against
yellow cottonwood leaves,
stands punctuated with fir.
Fall air crisp, potent,
calling out to the treed hill behind the track,
to shelters with deer in full rut.
Bucks listening, watching.
Velvet horns push their way
through red alder brush,
through rosehip and snowberry jewels.
The winding tracks no longer their territory,
circling the town.

Still the flag waves,
ruffles the grey lead sky,
salutes the parking lot —
open for business signs
inviting commerce.

Snapshots of Port Edward Cannery

We amble down the boardwalk,
smile like contented tourists
dreaming our stories.

history has a way of remaining silent

We peer into display cases
at manufactured antiques,
tobacco cans, enamel dishes,
wooden fruit boxes.

Purchase old-fashioned candy drops,
gold nugget bubble gum
from a Scottish storekeeper,
his thick brogue disappearing
between the tours.

He entertains with tales of adventure,
displays bounty —
Chinese green-tinted opium bottles,
a Japanese salt-glazed sake bowl,
dug up at opposite ends
of the cannery.

We purchase thin coiled
notebooks of local history,
the official version
of the growth of the town.

history has a way of remaining silent

A Japanese mannequin mends nets.
Paint-chipped face, unkempt wig,
thick woolen pants folded over.
She has no feet,
hunches over her nets
like a feral child,
frozen.

Black and white snapshots —
fish line the floor in a great
ocean of bodies,
assembly lines,
head and tails removed
day after day.
Bodies stagger off to bunkhouses,
their segregated sections,
do not mingle.

Not much left.
Portions missing like dismembered limbs,
buildings that housed First Nations
towed away then burnt,
structures for the Chinese
swept into the channel.
A Japanese net loft still remains —
its platform, a sliced off segment,
holds a tangle of nets
sprouting hemlock
with nowhere to grow.

history has a way of remaining silent

Nearby, homes for European families,
white like gutted halibut bellies,
stand in fine repair.
Fresh paint covering weathered timber,
a neat little row without the scars
of chopped off fingers.

Leaving Home

There are no rituals
for this shifting of place
in the landscape of mothering.
Only memories
like an overgrown field,
prickly burdock softened by
velvet wild rose.

I return to the hillside
where I waited each afternoon
eager for your stories.
Blond head emerging from the school bus
like the first dandelion
racing across the asphalt
to fit your small hand in mine.

There are no rituals
for letting go.
I long to kindle a fire,
stain my face with thimble berries,
weave daisy chains in my hair,
sprinkle devil's club into the flames.

My feet anchor to the earth,
roots reaching back into time
where I stand,
eyes never leaving that
stretch of highway.

Barbara Coupé

Prince George

The Ladies Dance

I am helium, stringless
in this arboreal atmosphere of rust
where the Ladies
flushed with auburn tresses
sway to a Beetle's tune

they sport spiked coronets of needles
twisted and transformed
into the fire-breathing chlorophyll of doomed beasts
a finality of crowns and canopy
sweeps and snags the sky

ah, the flying, falling melody of rice
wedded bliss of *Dendroctonus* and *Ophiostoma*
the Insect/Fungi Jug-band
playing the pitch pipes
and singing the Blues
the dying air stained
with the sharp scent of resin
and the saw-edged resonance
of chains and change

> *Economic calamity!*
> *Ecological disaster!*
> *Extinction of species!*

beat the drums of the band leader
while the Beetles bore
engorge on phloem pâté
and ignore the Pileateds
who feast on leftovers

undeterred, the Ladies dance
they spiral across this unmended landscape

in a vast promenade of pomegranate shades
a Red-Tide surging ever eastwards
on prehensile sound waves
that surf our milder, modern climes

but this I know

the music will mute
the dance will disperse
and the Ladies will languish
into faded crones who claw and scratch
limbs into the overstory
their silhouettes will stand
bent and stiff
sentinels to their own succession

contorted
they pine in silence
as nature begins
a different tune…

Red Clouds Dancing

For Cecilia DeRose who teaches the Shuswap language with grace and humour.

Cloud People
breathe red air amongst the trees
women dance in forests
struck by lightning
they wear feathers turned into fire
and stand tall against the sky

tiny beetles
play fiddles and make the pines cry
the trees sing a blue death song
and weep tears of pitch

Coyote beats his drum
while insects eat the inner bark
and do not see
fat woodpeckers looking for food

the people shout
      "Where is our food?"
      "Where are our trees?"
      "Where is Coyote?"

their women dance
spreading across this sick land
like patches of fur
falling off the deer, bears, and cougars
in the warm winters
of today and tomorrow

Coyote knows
that the dance will stop
the ladies will settle
become aged and stiff
in the black tree branches
that watch the changes to come

the elders still cry
while Coyote slowly
medicines their land
changing the song
and choosing a different drum...

Dormancy

this shallow curve of sun
silhouettes the branches
of the aspen clones
and breathes Winter into the atmosphere
it scrapes raw the questions and exclamations
lying dormant in the buds
those small tongues that cling
frost-frozen to playground posts
in a harsh embrace
of iron, arctic winds, and open mouths

in these low-light hours
the aspens can not speak
Winter, it seems
will never let go

The Question Marks of Ferns

Gymnocarpium dryopteris
Athyrium filix-femina
Dryopteris expansa
uncoil from the press of frost
and ask
    is it time?
    am I ready?
    will I be strong enough
    to unclench these fists of winter?
for snow still clings to hollows
and ice lingers in the shade of frowns

but look...

the former *Smilacinas* are starting to grin
and bunchberry has rebounded
even Devil's Club
has come out swinging
with piquant attitude

into this rare Cedar air
a whisper warms into a shout
the season is stirring
irrepressible, irrevocable
as undeniable as a nod to the sun
on a spring day

yes, it is time
and yes...
you are ready
to be strong

Marita Dachsel

Williams Lake/Edmonton

Main & Broadway

Immune to the pushes, the bloody screams,
you preferred to be coaxed out by a pack of firemen,
two pairs of paramedics. An ambulance idling,
confetti lights trumpeting your arrival.

The splintered wails of car accidents,
fools amplified by drugs or love,
the crashing waves of bus stop angst,
all impervious, continue their perpetual loop.

Your cries don't mimic sirens and you have suckled
on the exhaust of thousands waiting for the lights to turn
as we floated on our hardwood clouds, surveying
four floors above your concrete kingdom,

our faces mirrored in the window,
you nestled on my lap,
the traffic lights streaking in the rain.
This breath of time, a slow exhale.

The century-old dowager cradles us
in her faded brick apron, cracked concrete palms.

Presendia Huntington Buell

My ululations have scraped across this country,
my voice like fingers grieved to the bone,
leaving grooves thick enough for wagon wheels.

I would follow any man who promised our reunions,
who gave me no blame, who understood completely
when I sensed them

                     as shadows between the trees,
                     glints in the rushing brook,
                     the deer racing our wagon.

My back turned, I am a lunatic.
Stories of mine retold — the angels pacing,
my own children visiting — easy in lightness.

I repeat their names aloud: Silas. Thomas.
                        Chauncy. Adaline. John.
                        Presendia Celestia.

If I don't continue to mother them,
give their names breath,
no one ever will.

Silas, Thomas, Chauncy, Adaline, John, Presendia Celestia,
Silas, Thomas, Chauncy, Adaline, John, Presendia Celestia,
SilasThomasChauncyAdalineJohnPresendiaCelestia

My three other children have grown & left.
I still speak to my six, keep them close.
But they, too, have tired of me, give me no signs.

My heart is rutted like the prairie after frost.
I'd like to trace my finger along its deep scars, discover
where the furrows meet. Certain it won't be as simple as death.

Agnes Coolbrith Smith

A knitting needle pierces the prairie night.
I swaddle myself in my marriage
quilt & lumber outside
to a crowd of smug stars.

My belly, again, too heavy
slows me down. Oh to be lithe,
fierce in movement, darning
through the grasses to the edge.

I search for my husband
in the pinpricked sky. Can you see
me, Don Carlos? I miss your letters,
your poetry, your gentle presence.

You knew family was not easy
& sometimes neither was faith.
You must know I am to marry Joseph.
Your words no lullaby, a nightly refrain:

Any man who will teach & practice
the doctrine of spiritual wifery
will go to hell; I don't care
if it is my brother Joseph.

Once he is gone, yet another of your clan
will take his place beside this levirate wife.
Choice is an Autumn leaf. I am limp
with questions, no place in this world.

Do you know the difference
between faith & hope?
Do you know how to live
with one, but not the other?

I do. I do.

Fanny Alger

Emma's fired up.

Keeps complaining about how I miss the corners sweeping, don't move stuff dusting.

I try. I do. It's just so hard,
so hard to do anything feeling this way.
Lunch always rises up, lodged at the top of my throat.
I want to puke every breath of the day.
Or sleep.
But a hired girl can't sleep the day away.

I hate it when she's mad at me.
I love her. I do. I love her.

But Joseph's the one whispering in the middle of the night.
Sneaks in like a cat, hopping on my bed all hands & breath & mewing release.

I'd much rather be in her arms.
Not in that way of course, but you know. Like a daughter.

I wish I hadn't agreed to be his wife, 16 was too young.
It's been a whole year now.

God, just the thought of eggs makes me want to retch.

Marinda Johnson Hyde

& these are my tomatoes
planted 24 varieties this year
been collecting seeds, trading
for almost a decade

here I feel
         like a patriarch
fingers splayed, laying hands
blessing the rows

like wives, these plants respond
well to attention, a gentle sweep
of the leaves, tickle of the flower
& they won't stop giving

now,
        bring your palms to your face,
inhale
        oh, that smell

after all these years
I still can't find the right words
to describe their scent
                can you imagine?

Martha McBride Knight

The air smelled like honey,
the day warm & heavy.

I was bread rising
for thick hands to shape.

∽

Bed stripped, sheets rolled
around my fists.

My whitest linens,
my finest embroidery

witness to two marriages
consummated, two men loved.

Anguish, steam
scalding my throat,

I wanted the best
of me to cover him,

cloak his death.
Be the last to lay with him.

∽

I am not used to this,
how the land goes on forever,

chokes me with space,
its immensity.

I will never see New England again,
its ragged, stony hem,

the burning lace
of autumn.

Corseted in a life of exile.
Unleaven, caught.

Sarah de Leeuw

Prince George

∽

Travelling Three Lines

If at first it sounded like rain…
If you lead her to water…
If you drove here with toys in the backseat…
> From "Seated Figure with Red Angle (1988) by Betty Goodwin"
> in Anne Carson's *Decreation.*

Then, when together we first saw Betty Goodwin's *Seated Figure*
with Red Angle, we were 3 with her. We had travelled separately
to that room. To each other. Bodies in flight. Craving touch.

Then, before that, it was the first time I saw you. Seated. No
red in sight. But rain. In a wind city, oh the downpour of sound,
blood rushing into my ears. I had arrived. At you.

Then. 3 years later. City of running, nervous motion of confession,
maps of where from and where to. Me: a distant slippery landing
strip. Body of salty water. You: 3 children and toys on a backseat.

Then we embarked. Clutching plane tickets, train tickets,
steering wheels, highway lines and byways to hotel rooms
on roads going west to vanishing points ending. With you in me.

Then, afterwards again in flight, I am shattered
by turbulence. All separation and angles. Torn red as
rotting Elderberries. We fly apart. I feel cut. Like I am bleeding.

Then we come, together, drive these sharp-shouldered divided
highways beside each other. And I will drive you. Close.
In the sun and the rain, travelling to a point with no end point.

Then always. The rain and the bodies of water it makes. If not
today, sometime down the road. Freeway traffic shakes,
and makes, dry leaves. So let me be your rest. Stop. Water.

Then in the desert. Nothing but
the desert. Mirages on salt flats baking
in the sun, your skin shimmering wet.

Then you make roadside love to me beside
a tiny thin sage bush amongst the thousands of sage
bushes, full foliage on spiced sand singeing my back.

Then. Let's do that again. You
making love to me amongst sand and sage.
Mica indenting my spine. Hot sun haloing your head, sweat.

Then we cross 3 state lines: Nevada, Arizona, Utah.
Las Vegas to Bryce Canyon and back. Conquered by armies
of terracotta soldiers, sandstone snow, cold bright orange sunset.

Then the land fractures, again. Mirages, angleless ghosts seated
on asphalt. We drive through them, breath held, oblivious to signs.
Nothing but an open road, horizon, and mesas slipping into night.

Then 3 Mexican cowboys appear, white Stetsons in a white
pickup truck, a dream with tumbleweed. You touch my
knuckles, then my neck. Roads are a stretching woman's arms.

Then some days I awake. And stretch.
And. You. Are gone. Travelled home.

Then I become a Voyager, exhausted in my quiet home,
portaging from room to room to room. The weight
of your absence raw as shoulder blade bruises
left by balancing a canoe for days across my back.

Then visit me in the winter. Travel train tracks screeching
in nights of minus forty and falling. Setting sun and a full
moon by mid-afternoon, a din that is the deep deep cold.

Then breathe. Me. In. Jagged. Shards. Of air.
Lungs jammed like cottonwood sap underground in ice
soil, roots, and tree veins. Travel to my winter.

Then I will ask: Has throat singing,
breath transformed in the groans of an Arctic
tundra during thaw, ever moved you?

Then I will ask it again, this way: Have you ever been
overcome by the growls of two girls, clutching stretched-skin
drums the size of suns, inhaling each others' throat sounds?

Then, if you answered no, and if you
did not experience a quickening of heart, I will
know we may never travel like caribou. Hooves shuddering.

Then, if you answered yes, I will know somewhere in a
memory you may have forgotten, you carry the smoothness
of carved soapstone and the ecstasy of bears, dancing.

Then there will be glacier sand, ice deposited,
pockmarked by hailstorms in May when not
a single path appears possible. Not even one step further.

Then there are other moments too. With monuments. A church
with the blue light of Chagall's stained glass. Wooden bridges.
Over rivers full with swans. 3 testaments to our travelling, far.

Then, also, a lip of canyon, hiked to in a dusk full with
the calls and wings of young swallows learning to fly.
Fear no height. Do not talk about sorrow. Gulp back tears.

Then these too are our places. A forgotten servant's room, single
bed with blue sheets. Another bridge, steel girders, thronging with
tourists. I am seated. You wear a grey felt hat to kiss me. Brim.

Then herons, blue-grey wingspans, provide us direction.
Seeing two and the answer is no, east. Three
and our answer will be yes. Yes! West.

Then land. Land and settle upon me, a loon landing
on brackish rain-stirred sea water. That black tidal line,
your lonesome travelling cry.

Then our directions are also the bark of a coastal Arbutus tree.
Sweet smooth rust red peeling. You kiss me where I am
this tree's trunk, on this straight stretch of highway.

Then, when you finally arrive, the night will be quiet
and full. Crows, always loud in daylight, also sleep after
10:00 pm. They either forget to call out or there is no need.

Then distance will remain unsympathetic. To us
travellers. Even seated, resting and reposed, miles are red-mean
and harder than granite. We chip away at them.

Then once I drove toward a hope of you. My headlights caught
the eyes of a thin, thin, black fox. Glowing. But emaciated. Like
the scarcity of hours with you, he disappeared amongst fireweed.

Then these, oh darling my darling, are our days. Away,
mostly. Details lived. Apart. A ratio of less than 3 to 1. But
still, travel to me. I await your suitcases tossed beside my bed.

Pamela den Ouden

Fort St. John

Preemie

for my mother

not wanting to be plucked
from the world
where I floated
slung in a hammock

not wanting to chance
steel fingers around my head
bruising my brain
not old enough to know better
I came early

           2 lbs. 3 oz., my mother said

the intern leaning against the door
reading the newspaper
relax, he told her
it'll be a couple of hours yet
he didn't know me
but my mother knew
she reached her hand down
I felt her touch my head

           fell out, my mother said

a midwife from Indonesia
hands that held many
1500 babies felt her touch first
was there to catch me
wrap me in her body-warmed slip

           1501 babies, my mother said

later the doctor signed
confirming he delivered
the above-named patient
of a living female infant

wasn't there, my mother said

not wanting to be man-handled
I came early

Why I Don't Watch Movies

the sailboat capsizes
throwing the lover into the foam
shore was in sight
they should have made it home

or a chase scene — car forced
onto the bridge abutment
metal-concrete animal
leaps over the edge

or terrorists grab a blonde three-year old
her mother's hands bound
eyes blind under a black hood
bombs walls of fire
body parts airborne

or even something domestic:
a man slaps his wife
because dinner wasn't ready

the nanosecond when it could have gone the other way
but never does
hope escapes —
air from a popped balloon

When Famous People Die

the news is full of their stories
their birth
their rise to fame
from humble beginnings
   a father who was a baker
   a mother who worked in a cigar factory
   in a village that no one has heard of
their accomplishments
honours that are heaped on them
at their life's end
   others not wanting to miss the chance
   to recognize their greatness
their bodies are shipped to their hometowns
where they lie in state
thousands passing by to pay their respects
people are interviewed
who knew them when they were schoolboys
throwing balls through windows
or girls who babysat their children
we cluck and say *such a loss*

when famous people die
their agents email Associated Press and Reuters
confirm they were bravely battling this or that
no comment on their last moments

wives and daughters
second wives and lovers
sons and husbands
gather at bedsides in hushed rooms
holding hands
whispering prayers
or cursing and crying

Doctor's Orders

looking like Betty
from Riverdale High
or maybe a golden-haired angel
the oncologist
young enough to be our daughter
sits beside the bed on which my husband lay

she cradles his thin hand and arm
speaks gently *I'm sorry*
there is nothing we can do for you
go home with your family, love them
you have four maybe six months to live

she was wrong on both counts
it was two months

and there was no living about it

Forecast

the woman behind the counter
chats about the weather
as she takes my money
wraps my parcel
more snow tomorrow, she says
not caring about snow or no snow
I let my eyes drift to the shelf behind her —
a small blue ceramic jar:
 ashes of problem employees

it's a joke
I've seen others
 Harley fund
 boy toy money
 life savings

I want to ask her
what ashes mean to her

instead I think about the story
we read in class today
the hospital the mother
hiding the pain

I'd forgotten about the pain
the morphine —
the glass ampoule snapping
low animal groan
unhuman moan
round foreign sound from deep
somewhere where no one
wants to go
the twisting-away-from
never-getting-away-from pain
it makes me crazy

I want to tell her
what ashes mean to me

instead I think about the story

The Language of Trees

I have heard
trees speak their own language
laid my ear against the trunk of the maple
heard the sap murmuring sweetness and light
love songs for sleighbells and horses and snow
I have heard the willow wind-whisper my name
reaching for me with long fingers as I run past
trees have argued in my presence
branch-tongues clicking as they gave point for point
spoiled children stamping their feet and pouting
I have heard trees in pain weeping
great groaning at the loss of green
leaves *tsk-tsk*ing as they jumped unbidden
trees unashamedly crying a thousand leaf-tears
that layer-upon-layer create peated earth below
trees have laughed and I have heard them
such soft syllables tinkling
tickling my ear
trees whistle
a tune
at work
high
and
low
notes
singing
reciting
gossiping
Though not perfectly, I know the language of trees

fyre jean graveline

Prince George

ᔕ

Oh Canada. Our Canada. One of Four Against.

DRUM
FLUTE
SONG

September 13, 2007. History. in the Making.
a long time. Long Time. in the Making.
After over. 500 years of Colonization.
                    Worldwide annihilation. Genocide.
People. finally came. to the Declaration.
          Meeting. 22 years.
          Imagine. 22 years. in the Making.
Negotiating. Drafting. Redrafting. Satisfying. 143 member countries.
          The United Nations. Declaration. on the Rights.
                    of Indigenous Peoples.
          "a sign of the international community's commitment. to protection.
          of the rights. of Indigenous peoples" they say. [1]

DRUM
FLUTE
SONG

Since September 13, 2007.
The United Nations. now says.
          Indigenous peoples. have Rights.
                    Rights. to Self-Determination.
                    Rights. to Participation in Society.
                    Rights. to Freedom from Discrimination.
                              Hey! Anybody here ever win a Human
                              Rights Case? in Canada?
                    I never have. No One. ever does.
                    No Injun person. Anywuss.

78

DRUM
FLUTE
SONG

Since September 13, 2007.
The United Nations. now says.
    Indigenous peoples. have Rights.
        to maintain our Spiritual. Linguistic. and Cultural identity.
            Does this mean I can burn Smudge.
           and Drum in classes without being harrassed?
                Or get my trips to get Doctored by a
                Medicine Person paid for under Medicare or
                Blue Cross?
                    Or that Indigenous language programs
                    will finally become part of public
                    schooling?
                    Or every Canadian will have to learn
                    Cree?
                    The largest Aboriginal linguistic
                    group in Canada.
                    I doubt it.

DRUM
FLUTE
SONG

Since September 13, 2007.
The United Nations now says.
    Indigenous Peoples have Rights.
        to Lands and Resources.
            Wow. The end of clearcutting of Sacred Forests?
            No more digging up of Burial Sites for golf courses?
            This is Revolutionary.

DRUM
FLUTE
SONG

Imagine. Indigenous Peoples. now have the Right.
        to continued survival as Indigenous people.
        After generations of genocide.
        Loss of millions upon millions of Indigenous lives.

to mass murder and disease.
Loss of millions upon millions of Buffalo.
of ancient Trees.
of Salmon.
After millions and millions of dollars.
invested in Assimilation. and Extermination.

Imagine. We now have the Right. to Survive. as Indigenous Peoples.
We are Survivors. But. Buffalo.Trees.Salmon. may not Survive.
Our lives. Our children. Our Ancestors.
May Be. our Only. Remaining. BirthRight.

DRUM
FLUTE
SONG

But, wait a minute. That sad Tale. That sad, sad. Tale.
is Just the beginning of This Story.
That is, on September 13, 2007.
The United Nations Declaration says
Indigenous Peoples have Rights.
But. Canada. Oh Canada. Our Canada. is one of the four against.
Canada. Oh Canada. Our Canada. voted Against Indigenous Rights.
I heard the news. And I was Numb. I still cannot believe it.
Canada. United States. Australia. and New Zealand.

voted Against.
Oh Canada. Our Canada. voted Against.

Imagine. out of one hundred and fifty eight … member countries.
Only four voted against.
And Canada. Oh Canada. Our Canada. is One. One of Four against.
Four Against. out of one hundred and fifty eight countries.
After 500 plus years of colonization.
After 22 years of work. by Indigenous Peoples at the United Nations.
Oh Canada. Our Canada. Can you believe it? We. Voted Against.

DRUM
FLUTE
SONG

Oh Canada. Our Canada. Voted Against.
I am Ashamed. to call myself Canadian.

in the Indigenous World. Today.
Right Now.

For all. the Canadian History. I know.
And have Raged. and Cried.
Long and Hard over.
I have Never. been so Ashamed. to be Canadian.
"This is a stain on the country's international reputation,"
says AFN National Chief Phil Fontaine.

DRUM
FLUTE
SONG

And Canada. Oh Canada. Our Canada. is One. One of Four against.
Four. prosperous fourth world countries.
Four. have become wealthy off Indigenous lands.
Four. continue to exploit Indigenous resources.
turning Treaty Rights. into Wrongs.
Four. do not recognize Indigenous Rights to Survive.

Union of BC Chiefs Grand Chief Stewart Phillip tells it:
"It is truly ironic that the four first world countries that have become
prosperous through the exploitation of the lands and resources of the
Indigenous peoples, including Canada, chose to oppose the adoption
of the declaration."

DRUM
FLUTE
SONG

And Canada. Oh Canada. Our Canada. is One. One of Four against.
Home of the free and brave. Champion of equal rights.
states "significant concerns"
Yes. Concerns. for the rights of Whites.
Rights to continue to inhabit.
Rights to continue to prosper.
Rights to continue to rape Earth Mother.
No. Concerns. for how we must feel as Canadians.
as Indigenous Canadians.
Watching. Helplessly. as Stephen Harper's government.
reverses Ottawa's position. on the Declaration.

81

I have. Significant Concerns.
>When I Hear. that Canadian diplomats continue to work
>>in backroom channels
>>>to dilute the mandate of the Declaration.
>>Rubbing salt in now open wounds.
Yes. I have. Significant Concerns.
>When I Hear. allegations that Canadian diplomats
>>offered aid dollars in exchange for votes Against.
>>Joseph Ole Simel, coordinator of the African
>>Indigenous Caucus tells it: "By approaching
>>Africa, which had so many problems, and trying to
>>use aid as a tool, Canada was committing a crime."

DRUM
FLUTE
SONG

Yes. I.WE. have. Significant Concerns.
>Feel Scared.Sick. to be Indigenous Canadian.
>Home of Racist Back Room Negotiators.
>Digging. themselves into Bigger Holes.
>Trying. to dilute. Mandate. of United Nations.
>Crying. for Exemption. for being Against.
>Holding. poor African Countries Hostage.
>>All This. to sway votes against Indigenous Rights.
>>All This. to sustain Generations.
>>>of Impossibly. Unsustainable. Greed.

Yes. I.WE. have. Significant Concerns.
Feel Red.Rage. to be Indigenous Canadian.
Blinders. are Off.
>Boxing Gloves. are On.
Post-colonial. Canada.
>is a Myth.
Multicultural. Canada.
>is a Myth.
Neo-Nazi. KKK. Canada.
>Now that's more like it.

DRUM.FLUTE.SONG

Thanks Stephen Harper.
>for showing the Rest of the World

How it Really is. Here.
when you publically apologize
for the "sad chapter" of Canadian History:
the Residential School Genocide.[2]
And one year later publically announce in the G-20
meeting that Canada has "no history of
colonialism."[3]
Here. In Oh Canada. Our Canada.
where Indigenous Canadians. have No Rights.
No. self-determination.
No. participation in society.
No. freedom from discrimination.
Here. In Oh Canada. Our Canada.
Where Indigenous Canadians. have No Rights.
No Right. to Spiritual.Linguistic. Cultural.Identity.
Here. In Oh Canada. Our Canada.
Where Indigenous Canadians. have No Rights.
No Rights. to Lands. and Resources.
No Rights. to continued Survival.
as Indigenous Peoples.

DRUM
FLUTE
SONG

Unfortunately.
This is not New. News.
Here in Academia. We should know this.
Read Any history book. even the Colonial versions tell it.
Indigenous Canadians. have Never. been Entitled.
to any Rights.
Our forms of government have been outlawed.
Hereditary Chiefs dispossessed.
We have never had any real Voice.
in the governance of Canada.
Except for maybe once.
when Elijah Harper said No.
to the Meech Lake Accord.
Discrimination at every level is. Institutionalized.
Legislated. in the Indian Act.
Our Elders. were Jailed. for our Spiritual Practices.
Beaten for speaking our Languages.
We have had our cultural Artifacts.

Adornments. and Stories.

Appropriated. Distorted and Objectified.

Our Lands. have been Stolen. Raped of resources.

with No compensation.

We have been subjected. to all forms of Genocide.

including Mass Murder.

Same.old.same.old.News. History is.

DRUM.FLUTE.SONG

And through all of this. Five Hundred Years. of Genocide.

Oh Canada. Our Canada. has somehow maintained.

a "perfect" international reputation.

Imagine. A Perfect Reputation.

Well. the Real News. is finally out.

"Indigenous people in Canada must be going through hell,"

acknowledges Joseph Ole Simel.

Hell it is.

It is Hell. to be an Indigenous Canadian right now.

My hopes are Dashed. My illusions are Smashed.

Canada blew it. Blew their.our Chance.

Not. to be Perfect.

Nobody. is Perfect.

Canada blew their.our chance to show Respect.

To Respect. Indigenous Peoples Rights.

To Reconcile. our painful history.

To Resolve. to move forward together.

on the path of Human Rights.

Justice. and Development.

for all Canadians.

Not just the Rich.

Or the White.

Oh Canada. Our Canada. You scare me.

[1] All quotes are from p. 8 of an article published in the October 2007 edition of *Windspeaker, Canada's National Aboriginal News Source.*

[2] On June 11, 2008, less than one year after the vote against, Stephen Harper publically apologized in the House of Commons for the damages done through Residential Schools. Actions to reconcile and compensate for those living with the ongoing devastation this government policy caused, have been seen as too little too late and revictimizing rather than healing for many.

[3] On September 25, 2009, just over one year after his public apology admitting government responsibility for the legacy of the Residential Schooling Stephen Harper bragged to the G-20 international gathering of leaders about how good Canada has it, including "We also have no history of colonialism."

White Noise

kshkshkshkshkshkshkshkshksh.
heart pounding
blood surging
mouths opening. closing. opening. closing.

kshkshkshkshkshkshkshkshksh.
running headstrong. headlong. into a brick wall.
a totalitarian regime.
hurts my mind.spirit.body.

kshkshkshkshkshkshkshkshksh.
expendable. not affordable.
temporary insanity. money cannot fix.
no. and that is the last word.

kshkshkshkshkshkshkshkshksh.
white noise.
everywhere. overhere.
nowhere. i wanna be.

Shuuudddduuupp!

Jamella Hagen

Hazelton/Whitehorse

ဢ

An Introduction to My Mother

Scene 1: Bathtub

She's standing naked
in the bathtub at midnight, in her gumboots.
Beneath her feet, the submerged
pack rat trap: long wood box
with a trick door. Inside it, the rat
drowning. My brother sleeping upstairs.

Night ticks forward quiet as a child's
held breath, the light switched off, water
flat as a mirror — until the rat
untricks the hatch and springs out,
wet and mad and desperate.

Did they look each other in the eye
.before she started stomping?

Scene 2: Semi-Automatic

Her father wouldn't spend that money
on college, but after she left California
for Canada, took root in the bush
and had two babies, he bought her rifles
in case of bear attack.

Each time we visited, he sent her home
with another gun. At the San José airport
after he gave her the .30-06 for Christmas,
she wrestled a cart, both children,

that long grey case. The pile beginning
to shift. *Mommy, mommy, the gun's falling,*
I cried out as we approached the security lineup.

Scene 3: Broken Windows

As far as I know she only ever used the guns
inside the house. First a pack rat,
which she shot along with the window
of the backroom. That splintered mouth
gaped for years until she could afford
to replace the glass. Next the Saturday morning tomcat,
shot from her bedroom window at 6:00 am,
rocketing my brother and me from sleep.
But when the bears came, lunging slick
and drenched from the river, pushing their damp
black noses out of the bush and ambling
through the yard, she left the bullets
on that high shelf in her bedroom
and let them pass.

My Father Explains

That first winter
your mother and I had goats —
we lived upstairs in the bedroom
the goats lived downstairs,
that's why there are tooth marks
all over the living room walls.

We butchered once a year.
Afterward, I couldn't eat meat for weeks
but your mother
would run back, throw the bleeding livers
into the pan and eat them. You know,
you were always like your mother that way,
always liked liver.

After the Moon's Gone Down

I

Why is it when you're lonely you remember
    being alone? Or when you're stoned
all the memories of being stoned
    come flooding back? Suddenly,
you're lonely and stoned and sixteen
    wandering the dark with a boy
you hardly know, red willows brushing
    at your cheeks like hands, sounds
of a distant crowd sifting clear
    as church bells through the whip-red
branches.

II

And you're stumbling toward the outhouse,
    vomiting across the path. The girls
at the fire suck back Kahlua mudslides and laugh
    as you fall into a bush of ripe thimbleberries,
swear you won't hotknife anymore — you can
    still feel the burn in your throat, hot
sandpaper, the way you sucked it in and held,
    having watched grown-ups do it all your life.
You sprawl. You sprawl in the gravel and thimbleberries
    in the yarrow and stinging nettles and if you move
your face you'll be sick so you hold on
    with your whole body, to this ground, this mud,
this little hill above Pentz Lake while bone by bone
    the chill seeps in, and you sleep.

III

Marley holds the jar in his hands, says the peaches
    taste like tomatoes, and they do. You eat them
anyway. Also, a tray full of french fries
    a half-pan of chocolate brownies
and a bowlful of instant noodle soup. You like
    that you can eat as much as they can
and sometimes more. You like it when
    they're afraid of the bush in the dark.
You like them standing clumped by the fire
    with glowing amber bottles in their hands.

You hate them too. You hate them shit-kicking
      in cowboy boots, you hate the snuff container
rings on the back pockets of their jeans, you hate
      the ones who hate you for being smart
at school, for being skinny, for being uncool
      and you'll only take your pants off for boys
from out of town, only
      swim naked after the moon's gone
down.

Field Mice

They've been there all along. Tunnels
in spring, their bottom halves
lying like highways over the fields
after the snow has melted. You don't see
the mice — they've gone deeper now,
under the long grass — but you imagine
that heavy white ceiling, whiskers
pressed back, a cold scurrying.
And you find out your best friend's mother
is dying of cancer and you are going to leave this place,
like your heart, behind, and your father will move to Hawaii
taking nothing but his good shoes,
and the field will grow up with spruce trees
tall as chimneys, lonely as clock towers. The mice
will still be there. In winter, a metropolis of little feet
travelling in blind tunnels under the snow.

Leaving the North

I was known there for falling
from horses, hillsides, the tops of poplars
that didn't bend as expected but

snapped. I left that place
pulling burrs from my hair, nursing
scraped knees and a bad

habit of wandering alone
after dark. Wound up in this city
with four white walls and no way

to read them, streets dusky and
swarming, a little Plato,
a little Hobbes to fill up

the loneliness. Sports cars droned
past the windows and short,
brutish shadows slid like hands

up the walls of the cave. I went
to parties, evading sleep
and reason as long as I could,

which was a long time. Eventually
came down with a cough
I couldn't shake, got the feeling

that in this city if you split open
any wall, you'd find
something awful inside —

mould, asbestos, parts
of lost women. So many
were missing then. It was a record year

for rain. Water was a door
we went through each morning
and emerged from each night,

amphibious.

Lisa Haslett

Prince George

Carving Out

the disease process began
with echoes back to a womb
surprised at my presence
where mind formed a map of body
etching in breasts, hips, fingers long and lithe

in a garden one fall
you said forever
carved my name in a tree
slow slow sap sticking our fingers together

formulaic kisses turn
to jagged conversation
grows to diseased denial
and empty beds

a peculiar beauty,
the pruning process

the cut is slow, tentative
the muffle of winter's snow
frosts the moment between
decision and action —
the final separation comes
with a sharp rip

at the memory gate
pain will wring out a gasp
or leave you
unafraid of silence
thumbing your empty ring finger

The Distance Between Trees

He sucks and huffs impatience
like cigarette smoke
flinging angry words
that smack the side of my head
if I stand too near

I want him to go
back to his camp home with silent loggers
let us return to the rhythm
of our fatherless week

He flicks the butt
into the dirt by the pockmarked Bronco
red with the rust burrowed into its side,
shuffles to the shop —
his sanctuary of gear grease,
mixed gas and orange hand cleanser

I want to follow,
sit on the ancient snowmobile
(in constant state of repair)
kick my heels into the track
with all kinds of questions
about Cats, de-limbers, excavators
just to hear the low rumble of his voice
like a grader on gravel

Instead I pick up the discarded
butt still wet from his lips
put it to mine and try to imitate
the deep inhale

My pink girly lungs can't handle it

Fifteen years later
I quit smoking, come home
for a Christmas of falling
bug wood in the back forty
knee-deep in snow pushing tree
after tree after tree   tree   tree

The only time he breaks
the chainsaw buzz of silence
is to point out a snag
tell me heads up, push this way, watch out for that
the choreography of experience
falling away and yet
knowing exactly what to do

Fat Free

She is growing larger everyday,
feeding off insults,
devouring words;
with knife and fork,
or fistful by fistful,
stuffing more down and down,
only the sound of smacking lips
to accompany mastication.
Her untold story growls around inside her stomach
and she mistakes it for hunger.

Sometimes she tries on a voice at home
alone in her room,
listening for proper pitch and giggle
hoping to sound a little like Danielle from Home Economics
(now *that* is a voice that could tell her story)
but it never quite fits.
Nothing ever quite fits.

She writes her words upon her body
with indelible ink in cobalt blue
to match her eyes
(which everyone says are just *so* pretty).
But the words stretch and spread,
illegible and unintelligible and lost
in the folds and rolls

until finally she slips from her skin;
the sheath of misshapen, unformed
words left in a crinkled mess on the floor

and walks away.

François Lake. Autumn, 1992.

for Pieter

before, the kiss of this water
was sloppy and warm
against my calves
on stolen sunny days
tiny minnows returned
from my pail
to their shallow home

I still look for you here

now, cold-blooded
the lake licks
through jagged rocks,
tastes the tread of my shoe on the shore

you said the fishing is good
at the edge of fall
pushed the aluminum boat
out into agitated, grey water
char and rainbow flicked up
gulped the baited hook

the slip into winter
is as quick as a last breath —
you know it's coming
but you still fight

dad says there are some places
they cannot sound the depth
dark, deep regions so cold
a body would be preserved
where sturgeon curl
death in their gills

the Carrier called it *Nidabun* — Lip Lake
did they look out
as I do?
see the wide surface
gaped open
as if to gobble you up

Jacqueline Hoekstra
Terrace/Gibsons

Skeena floods again

River I grew up with
has risen and fallen many times
not just tied to the moon but pulled by the
sun's oars locked tight in the distant horizon
murky and teeming
she wills her way spills
past the concrete barriers
(as if we can keep her in).

Her path is set and no breeching is allowed here
there was once an orchard some ten acres wide —
so hungry that spring she leapt her trenches and ate all the apples,
plums and cherries.

Low-lying ditches just this side of the horse fields
have long since pushed their tongues
up to what might be dry land,
blowing raspberries at the listing fences.

Sump pump in the basement runs endlessly.

Entrenched, my mother says she will leave when they make her —
days of livestock (cows, pigs, horses, chickens, turkeys, rabbits, pheasants)
have long since gone
now only the vegetable garden and the bees she worries over.

Will the old farmhouse hold out?

Imagine it sailing on down the river —
that's how it arrived barged in the late summer
on her liquid waterway some 80 years ago
men poling the shallows.

And now that old farmhouse can finally break free
throw her skirts up in abandon
washed clean.

Fishing with my father

1.
Salmons of impossible size
silver and sleek, stilled in
inevitable journeys
even bigger than I,
slight seven-year old

Holding fast to the sides of the aluminum boat
fingers white cold and cramped
telling myself stories of being swept away down
rapids that shook my insides up

A relief

Doing as I was told
holding onto nets secured to orange buoys
listening hard for the sound of another boat
head down, ears straining

Fear and certainty climbing up my throat
holding on tight to trepidation
my father throwing salmon into the boat bottom —
sounds like children's bodies being thrown

Smell dark grey and lingering

As his accomplice I feared for him, for me
being caught, unaware that I was innocent —
no culpability when you cannot say no

2.
Exchampshix River fed by the Gitnadoix
so green like peasoup, thick like you
could walk across water, giant rainforest
cedars dripping constance

September long weekends lasting
forever, the cold, the wet the discomfort
the slap slap of black gumboots red-trimmed
hitting my calves, leaving indelible black marks

Fingers trailing the water, half hoping some
salmon would engulf me,
like an afterthought
we were left on a small river island or shoreline beside
river rocks that stayed red forever,
climbing last fall's deadfall tangles
balancing on the cottonwood beams
shifting beneath my feet

Not so worried about grizzlies or black bears

My father several shorelines away
my brothers complaining
"dad always gets the best spot"
my disappearing into the real wilderness
less dangerous than the familial one

3.
Grown-up of sorts, in Port Edward
anxiety over going fishing with my father
morning train trundling by, shaking
the house, leaves, my fingers,
fog as thick as snow covering every surface
I had too much wine and said I would go with him
out on the aluminum skiff onto the ocean's skirts

Dread like I was seven again,
swallow fear and feel it climbing back up my throat
too many memories of fishing
to take it lightly

We went to the ocean —
being here a testament to something
large and nameless moving leviathan beneath us

Because when the boat wouldn't start and the motor grinded uselessly
and my father was red-faced, yelling and swearing,
but not at me,
then some coiled yellow rope, stiff with age and strain,
finally let loose.

Old Growth

In the smoking years
the sawdust from the mill
lay ankle deep on the summer sidewalk.

I was sitting at his kitchen table
disenchanted with my trial run at sex.

His six-year old son and
eight-year old son
eating cornflakes.

At nineteen, barely filtered,
I told his boy to make a wish,
my fingers burning down close to the end of the match.

Such a sixty-year old shrug,
already the sawdust at his feet
covered the wings of his toes.

I couldn't be his mother,
here in the morning
frightened of the buzzing in his eyes.

All those fallen trees,
and see how fast
I run through the timber.

At Lakelse Lake I forget you again

After all is said and done, you remain the most tragic of memories.

Living and breathing and drinking me in and all those beers
one after the other drinking payday away long before it came
to fruition like me just leaving because it was all so strange but never
wondrous and I began to believe that I was in some way responsible.

Difficult to get past jesus and how if you came to me now I might
save a little of the boy you could barely remember but who I saw
lurking in the bottoms of your cups.

"Drink up," you said and the skull and cobwebs grinned
from your thin white arms, muscles playing a slow dance
in your throat and smooth arms and skin your chest a field
where horses graze and little boys might have played marbles
before the bones, before the teacher who taught you such pain.

Before the babysitter played hopscotch and kisses on
you, too — *like that* — I would have made it different,
like a christian girl could save your ghost
from being resurrected every day at 4:15
when you came home and popped your first beer.

Phoning me from Vancouver three years later, me with my
own little boy to save, you told me of the thin line you were
still walking this time armed with heroine.

Horses you wanted to run in your veins and I said "no," no for
the children you probably have, no for the man asking for change
at the liquor store, no for the little girl on the bus clutching her
rock in her fist, whose mother won't let her keep it.

I want to know that you are out there somewhere riding
fast and furious away from the past, from the history in these words.
I want you to know that someone is still here, remembering.

K. Darcy Ingram

Prince George

∽

So many years later

I picture you still skating, beloved Bauers
scratching uneven ice, your best stick in hot
pursuit of the puck out before you
dodging like some erratic hare, only to
be caught, tapped, pushed ahead and
caught again

The down jacket you got for Christmas
billows out in a red parachute of padding
against a bitter March dawn while you practice
scoring on the empty blue goal set out
front of your house like you have done
since you were seven

skritch, skritch   *SWISH!*
           tap, tap

I've always wondered if you had any
warning, if you heard a throaty groan or felt
your blades suddenly stick against a soft
patch, or did the ice just crack silently
and swallow you as your puck sped off
safely ahead

I know how your breath would have
sucked out of you from the cold, cold plunge
how your coat would have become
your anchor and the hazy water would
have dulled your cries like tears, shine
of your blades flashing in its dim depth

I still wonder sometimes if you surfaced
at all, if you got the chance to try to claw
your way back onto the lake's unforgiving
winterness, and if you did why no one saw you
struggling or heard your freezing pleas
for help before you sank forever

I knew you were gone the instant I heard
your mother introducing herself on the phone
"Is my son there?" and I couldn't say yes, I
couldn't wish your skates back onto their hook
or your jacket to alight sloppily on some chair
in her kitchen

It was your father who drove to the police
station after your mother called everyone
looking, and your sister unravelled behind her
bedroom door, instantly aged by guilt that
she'd chosen to sleep in instead of shooting with you
like she'd promised the night before

They figured it out: could see your velvet-black
puck standing lonely on the naked surface like
a tombstone, the ice around it a dull mysterious
grey while below the lake water churned and hid
your body from the surface and the burbot
swam slowly along the bottom

It took two days to retrieve you as your mother
grieved in front of a living room window
whose view she cursed — and they tried to hide it
as they brought you up, wrenched your saturated
young form onto a tarp so your clothing
wouldn't freeze to the winded ice

Bleak-faced under their masks, the divers
looked up to two white faces overlooking your
death like weathered fans in the losing bleachers
one crumbling like ash against the glass, the
other open-mouthed, screaming her
teenaged anguish

And I heard as they pushed you back onto
solid ice and dragged themselves out after you that
one of your Bauers — laced perfectly tight to
protect your weak ankles — cut deeply
into one man's wetsuit and set him to crying
and bleeding beside you

Just hours after the funeral, Julie and I went down
into your basement with knives and cut up your
· treasured net — silent and sweating I helped push its bars
apart until they broke — then heaped it into the back of
some mourner's pickup truck in your driveway
and covered the rubble with snow

Small bones

When I looked into her eyes, I saw clearly the torture
of nine thousand nights of torrential rain and
black lightning, walls drenched by the battery
of water, floors raked and lifting from the swells
that slowly, effectively took her over and coloured her
the same slate grey that identifies the calm, cool bottom,
like the silt-base of a river dam where boys
hang lines off the concrete edge to catch
the granddaddy their fathers had forever told them
was there lurking, the phantom fish *their* fathers
had told them about when *they* were young.
And so it goes that water begets rivers, drama begets
theatre, fish beget whales, and sadness begets a fathomless
imprisoned lake. I saw it all there in the silence
of her stare, behind lashes pale as daisies.

When I was ten, I saw a cluster of daisies overtaken
by flood at Mara Lake — the body of water flanks a ghost
town ripe with dust and whispers of fear and lives fractioned
by the search for gold, the castings apparent in each shingle,
each paneless window, each rag rumpled in the corner
of a general store long empty of anything but shadow.
But those daisies stood fully under water, the wet
choking life out of them while they claimed their beauty
and reflected sun with cream-white petals as guppies
curled through their leaves and daylight filtered down,
pooling like a halo — the same way halogen lights
at the midnight coffee shop collected on the tips of her lashes,
prismed against her delicate nose, and lit the worn enamel
of her teeth as she spoke of the dangers of the cold
that is winter, of the depth of melancholy that slid between
her blankets at night and gripped her like a starved hunter.

In a motion smoother than fog or the spreading rings
of a rock tossed in standing water, she reached with
slim fingers to push a lock of hair off her brow,
captivating me with hands thin as butterflies, fingernails
like the moon during harvests in summer and long
ember-coloured evenings in the months before snow,
each small bone caught in her net of muted skin and outlined

by veins shrunken with hunger. And I imagined a breeze
picking up sand in a ghosttown, alighting grains on a fantastic
journey to a lake like Mara, rimmed with weeping willows
whose branches trailed in the current, and that sand
wafting through waves and flowers and settling with silt.

Tears threatened while I studied the arc of her earlobes,
tracing with my sight the path of her jaw and the sweep
of her sunset hair, picturing the girl I knew she had been
and could still be, the one who would be sweeter
to her own touch, gentler towards her own soul, more
understanding of the flowing curves of her female form.
Anorexia held her away from me, a concrete dam between us
too large and thick to allow infiltration, salvation or
collaboration. I owned nothing strong enough to stop
the aggressor which turned her sight convex, her perceptions
larger than life, and her smallest curves the most grotesque
swells in a sea of skin too enormous for such a small girl
to live in comfortably. And so it goes that water begets
rivers, drama begets theatre, fish beget whales, and sadness
begets a fathomless, imprisoned lake. I saw it all there
in the silence of her stare, behind lashes pale as daisies.

In Montana

Our songman is a flashing silver kind
who will always please and never die;
whose vibrating songs are new all the time
honeyed lips, love and soulful eyes.
                    "Untitled," Archie Weller

Our songman is a flashing silver kind
vibrant as hummingbirds, hidden amongst
birch and aspen; uphill from battle
he dances, wolf tails dangling
necklace threaded on rose thorns.
He chants in shadow, melody
a stream, a breeze, a sapling; he

who will always please and never die
defines our dominion, giving black
feathers and a coarse call to
harbingers of our doubt, painting each
topaz and pearl fin that swims our dreams
to depths beyond our imagining;
he whose chorus is exactness, he

whose vibrating songs are new all the time,
his distance sits in our breast, a cancer
undiscovered, while his rattle and
drum sound softly across browned
fields, thin buildings, parched plants
which ached to grow with us
to delight in sun and moon; his

honeyed lips, love, and soulful eyes
watch pained as we forget the wolf's tail,
the porcupine's quill, the raven's feather
and the flower's scent, to cast our faith
into mirrors, reflect our lie.

Interiors

the lights on his tree go out. Yet we have seen
enough and heard enough: the secret of losing
listeners — did Browning never learn? —
is to tell them everything. We lose details.
                    "Venetian Interior, 1889," Richard Howard

The lights on his tree go out, yet we have seen
gibbons arc through that canopy over leopards,
orchids, barriers of physics and reason into annals
of imagination. How is it we have watched

enough and heard enough: the secret of losing
grip is at our finger tips, on tongues, in white
washed bellies. Extinction thrives, yet we idolize
fashion, bank accounts, live without being true

listeners — did Browning never learn? —
his technology produces photos we don't *see,* view
only for rich jungle-colours; images should haunt,
demand change: a picture's job

is to tell them everything. We lose details,
absorb into murderous caverns called progress,
finance trees falling in legion in forests half a world
away, their green glow choked by greed.

Donna Kane

Rolla

Visitation

So this is what comes of broken screens
and sitting in the dark. One minute
I long to be treasured, and the next
it seems I am; my blood decanted

into the thin glass of a mosquito's belly.
Its wings fly my cells past the porch light
and they glitter, a ruby glow part
operatic, part "skip to my Lou."

My darling, I'm diminishing and can't
feel a thing, not loss, not the splitting of
a soul. My blood takes off and nothing
looks back — all glitz and toodle-oo
and I never cared for you anyway.

Resonant Frequency

The loon pipes air through its throat
and the mineral in me hums like the rim
of a wine glass, a microwave oven.
And like a party crasher on her third merlot
I want in on the conversation, my blood
burning up with bird call and breastbone.
I want to say, *this tremor reminds me
of what I am.* It's hardly true. My bones
could be scattered on the opposite shore
and still vibrate to the cry of a loon.

In the Middle of Dinner

I don't remember who suggested it —
perhaps my sister as she passed the peas
or my mother while buttering a slice
of bread — or even, thinking back, which song
was playing on the radio but I know
I was as eager as anyone to
lay down my fork, push back my chair, and dance.
And it was good that we did, my parents
waltzing past the kitchen sink, my sister
and her husband toward the microwave
while the food went cold. It was good to hold
you, good to be held in a moment of *this*. Only *this*.
I tried to fix it in my mind while our
bodies kept moving, kept turning, kept time.

Epiphenomenalism

which is the claim that thought is unnecessary
to the brain, much like fumes from a rocket booster
or Brad's shakes from alcohol withdrawal
the time Barry and I picked him up from the plane.
Twelve hours without a drink, Brad's hands
shook so badly he couldn't light his Export A, his fingers fumbling
until the cigarette broke, the blunt snap
of the paper wrapper a piñata breaking open, bits
of tobacco on the collar of his coat. At a bar
with terry-towelled tables, Brad needed
both hands to lift a beer to his mouth — the bottle wobbling
like a spaceship at liftoff, the brain hunting correction,
the gimbal so strong foam spilled out the top.

Fungus Love

Let me be your honeytuft, your candle snuff,
your pompom, tinder, hoof. Let me wrap
my butter cap around you. Be my sugar, quench
your thirst. Say *tremella mesenterica*, I'll be
your exoskeleton. When raindrops fall in scarlet cups
or ruffle fine-toothed rims, our spores will rise
from coronets, touch silverweed and beetle's legs —
track ways of our scent. From mitosis to meiosis
let's hyphae proliferate, then say apple scab
and vomit slime, because it's not all chanterelles,
it's dead man's fingers, stinkhorn, stem rot, rust, and peach leaf curl.
Let's praise it all, but especially death, the stew of our saccharine walls.
Without leaf waste, mote of ant husk, carrion and dung,
there'd be no symbiosis, no mycorrhizal love. Our fruiting bodies
wake the dead, the dead from which we've sprung.

Bee

A bee grips the straps of a dandelion
and the milk-lined stem flexes
the way thought flexes with the weight
of an idea, vaults it into whatever
you name: a teacup, a doorknob,
a signpost whose metal face
is now pocked with rust, dinged
by last winter's snowplow.

Sabrina L'Heureux

Dawson Creek

Car nap

The day we arrived
the road spun wet through
green hills and hayfields.
The buildings like so many dice
tossed into a shallow dish.

Here, the grass breathes quickly
before the crust of snow,
the fields in hibernation until summer.

As if I went to sleep
and someone buried my mountains
filled my lake in with hay
turned off the rain,
painted white stripes
on the crows,
and called them magpies.

No more bicycle streets
or row upon row of Tercels,
shiny two-doored thumbprints
next to the fists of 4 x 4s.

Here, the shadows on the valley
fall from the clouds,
not the buildings,
and when I sleep
the only sound is the distant
groan of thunder,
and the occasional rumble
of an oversized truck forcing
its way around my corner.

Here, people are struck more often
by lightning than by cars,
the buses are counted on one hand,
and every road
leads out of town.

What I'm left with

for nonna and nonno

Rare eyes: passed down
like hand-painted china, each grandchild's
a shade of moss, olive, deep green.
Recipes for meals I couldn't pronounce; biscotti, polenta,
plump balls of gnocci. The tradition of ten-dollar allowance
and bags of loonies on birthdays, saved
from trips to the Woodwards cafeteria.

The black and white photo of their wedding day:
pale skin, lips tinged with pink someone added on
with careful hands. The front garden roses, cut
into a crystal vase, petals the colour of nonno's wine,
the scent strong as nonna's bath powder, the quilt on her bed
dusted with a fine sheen of white from our tiny hand-prints.

The way my hands move, like nonna's: floured, firm,
a sculptor of bread hunched in rolls under a blanket,
like her own rounded shoulders, disappearing
into the folds of her silk floral blouse.

A bowl of languages: English folded into French
with Italian endings stirred in. English learned
from soap operas and romance novels
traded in at the second-hand bookstore for more.

And stories, like a box of moth-eaten sweaters
that I will wear every so often when I am cold
and think of nonna with a baby in Africa, her first home,
or nonno, miles away at war, waist in the trenches,
or the two of them years later,
singing *fait dodo* while I close my eyes

Weighing poetry

You asked why poetry
was so important.
Now, I'm on the scale
and you pass the anthology
of forty-five Canadian poets.
Suddenly, I weigh three pounds more.

Next, you pull
my Billy Collins from the shelf
a flimsy paperback
that doesn't even budge the needle.
But my Yeats, the hardcover
with gold trim, adds
another pound to my body,
and *The Complete Works*
of Elizabeth Bishop
adds two more.

Hard to believe
so many words
could weigh so little,
although I point
to the necessity of having
a particular slice of moon,
whether hoofprint or thumbnail,
two apples on a cold window sill
the warmth of lint peeled
from the trap,
or the girl I wrote of,
with orange rind beneath
her fingernails.
But still, your eyes seem to say
look, nothing. I watch
the needle waver on the scale;

with all I hold,
how light
we still are.

Dance Partner

Up close, the tree is carved for climbing;
each branch, groove, woodpecker hole
a new step. Her fingers clasp
thin branches; her feet tiptoe
higher. The branches spring back
when she lets go,

a shower of needles drops,
drifts to the earth and she balances
on one pointed foot, shifts to the other,
step ball change, spins up another branch
and ducks a clump of pine cones.
At bare spots she wraps her legs
around the trunk, presses her cheek
to the rippled bark, and pushes upward,
careful *plié* to the final bough,

where one arm hugs the trunk,
and the other arcs above her head
as she bends, ankles crossed,
feet perched on their branch.
She swings one leg back,
lets go of the trunk,
and the needle-laden branches,
like layers of crinoline,
scratch her bent knee, brace
her body, hold her,
in *arabesque*.

Ode to tea drinkers

Sometimes I wonder
if you can tell a person
by the tea they drink,
the way flip-flops
versus red pumps
or Tolkien and Jane Austen
meld a personality
like the sun melts
a silhouette into shape.

In my hand, the pomegranate
green tea says, this town is too small
close your eyes
and see the city.

Orange pekoe is for those
who drink tea from bulk boxes
almost an afterthought,
while Earl Grey says "traditional,"
the striped bow tie
of tea, the old standby
with a desire to dress-up.
It wishes secretly to become
a London Fog, sipped in cafés,
earn a spot of its own
on the menu, next to the smoothies
and the French vanilla café.

Deep Roiboos sucks in the drinker,
fooled by a name so inflated and round,
it won't release you
until every syllable of its flavour
is drawn in like pipe smoke.
It resonates on the tongue
like the beat of a drum
held warm in the hand.

And even-tempered chamomile
whispers to its drinker,
the romance reader on the couch,

one dog-eared love story
flopped on its side,
or the man on the front porch,
bare toes curled against chipped paint
as he watches the dandelions march over the yard.

Caroline Lowther
Vanderhoof/Vancouver

Alterations

I was once a competent young lady
who knew answers
to questions long forgotten
cooked for haying crews
mixing harvest with slaughter
and never doubting the outcome

now I search books
on how to cook pasta from Safeway

I travelled across Canada by train
seeking adventure
eating graham crackers and cheese
while laughing with strangers
and crocheting a black and white afghan

now I pause at Kingsway
waiting to be hit

at 20 I hitchhiked
the length of BC with a dog
singing "Me and Bobbie McGee"
perched high in the cab of a semi
and slept under the dark fir trees
in Manning Park

now I lie awake at night listening
and plan traps for home invaders

I sewed my bridal gown of white satin
and then transformed it to a lace minidress
stole the pantyhose
from my sister's protesting legs
knowing all eyes would be on me

now I wear a bra 2 years old
with the wire missing in one cup
I am afraid the salesperson will ask me
if I need help
and I don't know the answer

Mary MacDonald

Prince George

ᔕ

Paddling Bowron Lakes

This I remember:

floating on wings of water deep, dark,
here now closer to shore, forests of wet weeds,
opalescent leaves in sun through water,
bending to the wind or current,
the tracks of bear and moose on the still-wet sandy shore,
and the white-belted kingfisher following
our canoe on its silent path,
hovering and dipping by the shore,
for the little fish.

The shiny orb of moon and
barred owl delicately threading its call
into silent cloth of night
wolves howling an ancient eery pack song in the distance,
voices blending into sky as they move away,
into the forest
where the mountains are.

Where the mountain creatures are,
we hear wing sounds
of eagle flying low against the dark strong tree limbs of shore,
Canada geese taking flight as chill nips the morning
through rain, thunder, lightning that flashes to our shore.

Salmon move like blood through water,
at the end of the lake near the shallow creek
fighting for life, spiralling, spawning,
the few survivors who made it this far
up the Bowron.

Wet skin with scratches,
soggy band-aids, bug bites,
finding shelter under a blue tarp with hot chocolate
against the chill of rain,
playing checkers and parcheesi,
sitting on stumps in rain pants
and pondering the trees.

Squirrels overhead with pine cones,
tossing bits onto the ground,
chattering to each other,

Fall is upon us,
the gathering time.

The bears are following the salmon.
They have left the blueberries
under the dark stick dead pines,
and we eat as many as we
can, in the wet chill,
bright red rosehips.

A splash in the water,
a glint of trout, a loon's call
follows itself down the waves,
becomes millions of loons who have gone before,
wings following the wing path,
through the water,
through the sky,
across this fluid world
where now we float,
becoming more than human life
of trucks, railways, machines
on the other side.

Huddled in the night tent,
under down sleeping bag,
bear spray close at hand,
just in case,
knowing we are creatures here,
just another set of footprints down the
still-wet sandy shore.

The journey that you are

to the trail, down by the lake,
where the moon lights a route of silver
across the water,
calling you to the centre,
to the other side,
up into the lighted lantern
of the sky, warm glow against
watery chill where we could walk
if we refused to drown

and down to the streets
of cracked concrete, scraggly dandelion,
Tim Horton's ragged brown plastic coffee lid,
oil rainbow in a puddle, stained corners
of sweat and desperate urine
where we can't even be bothered
to put up an outhouse for the transients
to piss in, swear words scrawled,
misspelled in red felt pen,
and you walk by ghosts who look at you
from cut up faces and empty eyes
and yell "fuck you too"
in your general direction

and to the ambulance call on the highway
where you need to tell them
she is dead, then to the morgue to hand a baby stillborn
in a little blue shoebox to an almost mother
who will take him home to bury
and to the soccer field where he scores years
later, and everyone stands and cheers

and all these places, I tell you,
you will go but you must not linger for there is more
to see on the path that you become as
years go by and you wonder where the hell
has the time gone, and what the hell
have I been doing anyway,
and you take another drink,
change another channel,

send another email out to cyberspace,
wherever the hell cyberspace is,
you don't really know, but it is in the centre
of somewhere

and keeping the Christmas tree up for half the year
and turning your electric light into a sunset with a burlap sack
and understanding that we are in outer space after all
and you will avoid the black holes
because you have more important things to do,
like sewing that new pair of curtains for the camper van
and making gooseberry jam like your grandmother made
and learning to two-step like you are floating
and touring England's castles
and cutting down trees
and climbing trees to save them
and crying
and laughing
and not knowing whether to cry or laugh when
everything has fallen apart
and the pizza you ordered
just landed with a messy thud on the floor
before the dog licked it up
because I say to you

it is a disaster out here
and nothing ever works out anyway
and you know you are a goddam loser
and the most brilliant child that ever was
who they talked about on the church steps
after you'd moved away to the big city and made a name
for yourself as a big shot,
and here you are by the flames shooting up into the sky
hitting the stars by the witnessing trees,
and somehow despite it all, you are
beginning to think — just maybe — you really can walk
this silvery trail across the water
to the other side

Pua Medeiros

Prince George/Hawai'i

Skun Gwaii

Hours of rough travel in a Zodiac
Skipping across concrete waves
Brought me to a place of wonder

Some call it Anthony Island
After God-knows-what whiteman
Others mistakenly call it Ninstints after the last chief
But the people call it Skun Gwaii

A surprising number of visitors from around the world
Trod that remote place
But I wondered how many heard the voices

As I stepped out of the forest
The English tourist voices were quickly overwhelmed
By old Haida voices

As I walked past fallen house posts
And weathered leaning poles
I heard the voices of women talking and laughing
As they worked together on the shore
I heard the children splashing and playing
In the shallow waters of the bay
And I knew the men were absent
Hunting sea mammals in nearby waters
If they would have asked me
I would have joined them
In their world

The people of so long ago
Came to life for me
So suddenly and so tangibly
If I had more time among them
I could have learned their names

I could have heard their stories
And learned the fate of each

I know diseases took them
The few remnants moving on
But they returned among the living
That day I walked on Skun Gwaii's shore

The Object

He remembers his great-grandmothers
Dancing to cure the sick and injured
He remembers they took him with them
He did not know why

He remembers how old they were
And how they died
One after the other
No one danced to cure the sick after that

The world spun crazily
Became unrecognizable
From the one he was born into

Every spring the high water
From melting snow and ice
Spring rains
Brings new gravel to the point

Spring brings mud too
Mud on the road leading to his new house
Mud on the driveway where he parks his new pickup
The wagons of his childhood are gone

A truck brings gravel for his driveway
Gravel the spring flood waters provided
His young son watches the truck unload
The boy spots an object
A smooth round flat black stone
With a square hole cut in the middle
Mom, what's this?
I don't know, Son.
No one knows
But son, mother and father
Sense it is important

Son believes The Object is his
Father takes it
Treats it carelessly
Shows it to his drinking buddies

I ask
Where's The Object
Father doesn't know
Son says
It left

Several years later
Looking at old photographs
Of *halid'm swanasxw*
Indian doctors
I see The Object
Hung about the neck of the healer
Atai'asxw
No English word for The Object
Object of power
Object representing the power animating the healer
His power to cure
To find the lost
To predict the future
To help the people

The boy was right
The Object left
It was there to bring a message
About the boy
We know about the father
That's why the old ones took him
When they danced
The boy has the power too
But the old ones have all died
The powerful ones are all gone
Leaving the boy
His father
And others like them
With that unrestrained power
Ricocheting around inside them

This Morning I Complained

This morning I complained
I can't afford to replace my five-year old car

This morning I complained
About how much tax came off my paycheque

This afternoon I went downtown
To get $200 from the bank
To spend on the weekend

I passed three poor-looking native men
Sitting on a bench in the hot summer sun
I though about how much I hate being thirsty when it's hot

I drove to the 7-11
Bought juice and food for three

I brought the food to those men
They were kind and grateful

The man I had assumed drunk
Was disabled
From a severe accident years ago
His uncertain walk
Had resulted in a fall
His arm was dislocated

He and his friends had just sat there

Not asking for help
Knowing they'd receive none

If I had assumed him drunk
What are the chances the white citizens of this town would too?

His name is Raymond
He smelled sweet and clean
Like reservation grasslands

I left Raymond at the hospital
With tears in my eyes
For him and all our other broken brothers and sisters

And for myself because I do so little

With Your Silver Spoon Shoved Firmly Up Your Ass

With your silver spoon shoved firmly up your ass
And absolute certainty in the righteousness of your position
You humiliate me in front of others
For the grave offense of making you wait two minutes
For your profoundly important work
With my so-called, by you, work

All wrapped up in that short exchange
Was a history of colonialism, oppression and Western superiority
The certainty of your belief in your supremacy over me
Was crystal clear

I wonder how conscious you were of all that lay behind your words?
I wonder if you know how insignificant a threat I am to you?
I walk in your world
At the peril of the kind of indignity you dished out
I can't play your game
I'm not well-armed enough
I don't have the language
The attitude
Or the certainty of dominance
So you get to violate me once more
You call me "uncivil" in your upper-class accent
Don't beat around the bush
Say it!
Uncivilized
Barbaric
Savage
That's what you really mean

Let me guess
When I'm not around
Like others before you have said to my face
You look down your nose and say
The product of affirmative action
Are you aware that you have actually looked down your nose at me more than once?

Can you possibly imagine what it took for me to get here?
I had to do all you did and much, much more

I came from a place of illiteracy and addictions
Of cultural differences which I apparently do not yet fully understand
I had feelings of inferiority to get over which I obviously have not yet fully overcome
Do you have any idea what the journey has been like?
When was the last time someone refused to rent you an apartment because of the
colour of your skin?

Don't worry, though
You can be reassured that I am still not where you are
Nor will I ever be
I am not willing to play the game you play
At the expense of others
You can rest assured that they pay me half as much
And I probably work twice as hard
Feel comforted by the fact that I have a half-dozen dependents to support
Never get vacations
And there are plastic lawn chairs in my dining room

Be reassured by the realities of my life
I'm no threat to you
Don't worry
I came from the rez and the ghetto
And I still live in those places too

Coyote and the Anthropologist

Coyote was walking along
When he came upon a man who obviously wasn't from here.
The man said, "Ah, Coyote, I've been asking these elders
About the nature of Coyote.
I am attempting to write the definitive work on the Coyote character."

Coyote wasn't sure what "definitive" was but he said
"Well, I should be able to help you with that.
Coyote is the exponent of all human possibilities.
He embodies the moral ramifications of our thought processes,
And he actualizes the dichotomous relationship between man and nature."

The anthropologist was impressed.
He had a brilliant career-enhancing thought.
"Coyote, how would you like to co-author a paper with me
And come up to the university to present it at a scholarly conference?"

Coyote thought about that for a minute.
"Yes," he said, "I will."

Well, Coyote and the anthropologist went to the big city to the big university.
They worked on that paper until it was perfected.
The anthropologist was really excited and anxious,
Looking forward to the awe and admiration of his colleagues.
It was such a coup to actually have Coyote there to co-present the paper.

The day of the conference came.
The anthropologist had arranged to present last
To increase the anticipation.
Coyote listened to the first presenter.
He fidgeted through the next one.
He snoozed through the next one.
And half-way through the fourth one
He whispered to the anthropologist
He was going to the bathroom.

The scholars droned on and on
But Coyote didn't return.
The anthropologist was getting worried

When suddenly there was a commotion outside the room.
The anthropologist went to see what was going on.

He found the buffet table in ruins
Coyote muzzle prints in every dish.
He encountered a matronly female colleague
With Coyote paw prints on the butt of her dress.
He found a big pile of stinking, steaming Coyote shit in the middle of the floor
And no Coyote to be seen.

At last, the anthropologist understood the true nature of Coyote.

Sheila Peters

Smithers

≈

The Buttercup Poems

Buttercup's christening

We could have named you dandelion —
but you are a cup
of sorts and I was afraid a bear
would read you wrong — plant his big black bum
spring scruffy on your upturned hull
and scrunch down into you —
stuff your splintering fiberglass
into his indiscriminate mouth
the way he does out back
when the canyon is yellow in June.

Buttercup waits

Take her out we urge our friends.

But when we come home
our travels over for another year
there are cobwebs on the life jackets
and a wasp's nest strung up inside the bow.

It's his elbow I tell her
from too much wood splitting. It's her
shoulder he whispers to her yellow
spine. She curls into the back wall
of the barn. Silent.

Promises promises

It has been at least two summers
maybe three
since Buttercup left the barn to go out
into the light the three
fireweed shoots reach toward each August —

141

purple in the gloom of rusting Tonka trucks
and abandoned seed trays. The dreams of bees.

We hope — a beginning — that we can manage
the lift up onto the roof rack. We do
and tie her down. Slip a finger under the gunwale
to scoop out needles from that other
summer she spent — hopeful — hopeless —
under the spruce tree. By the time we drive
out of the canyon it is raining. Fools, we say.

Buttercup hums a splattering tune
a we-shall-overcome sort of song and
we keep going out
and around
and behind the Babines
the rain pattering and the wind
shivering big cottonwood leaves to the ground.

Yes, it's September and we're taking
Buttercup for a drive. She keeps the rain
off the windshield so we promise
we won't turn back. We'll find a lake
and lift her off as best we can without
dropping her. We promise. We'll tear a part
of ourselves first. It's your turn, Buttercup.

The rain stops. The wind falls.
Buttercup is silent. She doesn't like
heroic measures.

We find a tiny lake where there's a car
and silent tent. It's noon and four bright
white running shoes are parked against
the zippered flap. The sun turns
the green reeds ringing the lake
the same new green the aspens turn in May.

We get her down — we do — and set her
in the water. Lap lap lap the tongues
talk and taste her peeling yellow paint.

She holds the water back and makes a pocket
to receive our awkward limbs. She
is quiet and the tent is quiet and the lake
is quiet. Any loons or grebes or mallards
have bred and fledged and gone and even the lilies
have hopped off their pads. We too are quiet
as we paddle out into the light.
The plants the insects the fish
all live together. Buttercup speaks to them.
She is light and she is heavy. She nudges the reeds
and they talk back. We float together.

This lake is not a tidal thing. Here is the land
and here is the water held in an ancient pocket
a glacier made before it withdrew to its hermitage
in the mountains. Most sunny afternoons it forgets
its vows. Slips down old paths to say its prayers
in congenial company. As we glide past, the glacier
looks down and says: Hello, Buttercup.

When we come home
we lift her off the roof
more deftly. We set her down
under the spruce tree.

Buttercup now

If it freezes tonight, Buttercup,
forgive us. We have been made fickle by peaches
and huckleberry picking. We will tuck you
in the barn before snow falls. Promise.

Or we could hang you from the living room ceiling —
a winter sun — lower you when the waves
break between the couch and the comfortable chair —
climb in and drink singing songs.

Sometimes at night, like you,
he lies on his side —
clears room for me in the tangle of forgotten ropes
and life jackets — shelter.

Some nights we turn our backs —
the smooth curves made fragile
by the empty places inside. When this happens
it's good to look out the window and see you
under the spruce tree — your extra paddle tucked up
under the seats and the bailer neatly tied inside.

A river lament

Poor river

mud and stone
concrete dammed
cottonwood snagged
and beaver log jammed
you generate clichés for village gossips
        and well-meaning friends:
                letting go
                floods and *sweeping everything*
                away.
They *will* step out to cross uncertain ice
        and lose themselves.
They *will* build their shacks on your flood plains
           and stand as if surprised when the clay banks
              slump into spring
              runoff.
They *will* launch their boats into your currents. You can see
        the figurative traps:
              sucked under
              spit out
              washed up.

              They want to be *washed clean.*
              Left breathless.
              Panting.

Even when they lift their paddles
and relax, tired, into the slow and circular sweep
of an unexpected eddy
          we know, river,
          they're already picking their next wave —

flipping their paddles to the other side —
we know, river,
they're already missing your turbulence.

Buttercup sets me straight

In a tangle of fishing line
cast by some autumn angler into a low branch of cedar
lures chime above the frozen river. The knots
are sticky with flesh snagged from some sockeye
on her way to the Babine — skin already black
pale patches decomposing
belly heavy with eggs.

I have felt them, Buttercup tells me,
tail slap my hull when they breach.
Nudge my keel when I get too close
to their gravel. Bears intent.
Eagles fat in the branches.

When you sing of *breathless*,
Buttercup says, of *panting* —
well, she says,
you have no idea.

Rebekah Rempel

Rolla

∽

Cowbirds

Every spring they built nests
in the combine. Sometimes baby birds fell,
landed among last summer's dust, wings still wet
from the shell, eyes blue and sightless as saskatoons.

My sister rescued them, cupped each bony body,
picked chaff from their new feathers.
She tucked them among grass and twigs
in a shoebox, knelt on the floor to feed them
crushed-up worms through straws,
their throats flickering.

When they died,
I helped her bury them
in the clay by the dugout, marked their graves
with crosses made from popsicle sticks.

Only one survived. Afraid it wouldn't learn
to fly, she crafted a cowbird puppet,
flapping the felt wings of her fingers
around the watchful head.

One morning we found it looping the kitchen.
It slipped out the open door and my sister followed —
running across the yard,
as though she too might escape the ground.

Frogs

When tadpoles swarm the marsh
I cup and fill my hands — so many lives
glide through my fingers.

Imagine we began here — this mulchy womb,
caressed by weeds as we grow our bones.
Sleep to the fibrous song of frogs
creaking through the murk, a rusty hinge
between day and night.

When it's time, we crawl through the mud —
our warm-blooded mothers waiting in the reeds
to wash the green from our cool skins
and carry us into the world.

I Breathed Deeper, Trying

The living room walls pressed
against my brother's reckless breath —
head tilted back, mouth open,
while asthma wrung the air
from his lungs. Lamplight
splashed across his face, everything
distorted, as if underwater.

I breathed deeper, trying
to show him, but only seemed
to tug the furniture and wallpaper
closer — would've blown
all my breath into him
if his airways had let me,
each the span of a grain of sand.

At the hospital that night,
I pulled the pale green sheet
to his chin, tightened the band
of the oxygen-fogged mask,
still felt I was leaving him
to drown —
tubes tentacled around the bed,
the sonar beep of monitors
bouncing off my back as I went.

How to Honour the Dead

Remember sitting on your grandfather's lap,
cold shirt-snaps pricking your back.
Think of those gospel choir tapes he played
after dinner, the Abbotsford Male Chorus.
And the silver tea set his parents smuggled from Russia,
the things you weren't allowed to touch, each cup on the mantel
a cool, polished well of history.

Remember the manure-musk on his coveralls
and swells of hay toppling from the loft,
sun a tunnel through the window. Remember
pitchforks hung on bent nails, tines soaked
with light. How he showed you exactly where to stab
a bloated cow — left flank,
an open hand's width behind the last rib.

Forget the milking hoses,
your father's skin splitting into welts
and the belt your grandfather took from a drawer one day —
the one he'd saved for decades, the one he broke
on your father's back. Offered it to him,
pieces hanging between them like a snake's shed skin.

Forget how your father knelt on the bedroom rug that night,
weeping, and your mother rubbed his shoulders —
like his own mother did with thick homemade salve.
Forget pain when the dead do not deserve your honour,
forget flesh, forget revenge. Remember light
breaking through the barn, one baffled swallow
hovering against a window — as if that were the way out.

My Mother's Hands

Purple scars criss-crossed
the tender insides of your arms —
X's and V's — as if you were a child
practicing the alphabet
and sketched your favourite letters
on your skin.

Those same hands held a buttercup to my throat
in front of the mirror — a yellow shadow —
as though I'd swallowed the sun.

When you pushed me on the swing set,
hands melding to the small of my back,
the clean sky sealed us within
our own world — one that I thought
could save you.

I never saw you knit or knead bread
like my friends' mothers did, but
you guided my hand as I learned to write.

Once, trying to understand,
I drew on my wrists
with red pen, hid the lines
inside my sleeves — a secret
we could have shared. Such things
your hands have done.

Laisha Rosnau

Prince George/Coldstream

A New Kind of Fire

We are recently domesticated, still surprised
how the shape and heat of our fear
has shifted and followed us, sullied
the house with the smell
of meat, metal, wet cotton.

Our fright was once reserved
for fiercer things: being alone
on mountains cloistered in fog,
rides snagged from roadsides, currents
that cut our ankles with their hidden edge.

Danger now loiters in each split-level,
throws curveballs down every cul-de-sac,
ricochets off garage doors, is speared
on the tips of fences.

But no, that's not it. It's us.
We don't fear the trappings,
we fear ourselves in them. It's okay —

we can still laugh about it,
backyards splayed with mottled shade,
drinks hard enough to wait until noon, soft enough
to seem harmless. Our children barefoot

in grass speckled with broken glass, unseen,
light sliced on imagined edges.

Our husbands joke about the skittishness of flame,
the barbecue's unpredictability, and we see
fire balls like second suns or entire constellations
of new planets dotting the backyards of our subdivision.

Bolt

I hadn't been on a horse for twenty-one years. Instead, I'd bucked
boys off me on the bench seats of pickups, dropped out of high school,
shucked off jobs like bad outfits, backpacked bug spray, journals,
thin clothes and thick sweaters from country to country, came back
with cheap silver and film canisters of sand. Eventually,
I eased into the ride, memorized postal codes, married a man
because I wanted to smell the back of his neck forever.

And then, I'm on a horse on some northern back road, moose stamped
on the crest of the hill like a figment of Canadiana, and the horse bolts.
I hold on even as I miss the girl who would have let go — crack of helmet,
broken clavicle worth that moment of air, body ready to forget its weight,
ready to remember it again, the road coming up heavy to meet me.

Hard Won

Milk pumped into bags, cycles
from cold pack to freezer to fridge to bottle.
I'm told the baby doesn't always refuse,
has a fickle relationship with disembodiment.

My body wants the baby, wants the baby
bad, breasts hard and sore, release far more
of a hassle without her, the apparatus awkward,
cold. We each carry something that smells

like each other, the baby and I. A comfort
for her, a cue for my body to produce food
in her absence. I can pump with one hand,
write with the other, though both wrists cramp.

I plug seventies rock ballads into my ears and shake
out my arms. Door closed, blinds drawn, bottled milk
still warm, I dance, a baby blanket cut in two
the thing I clutch as I let out a mute howl

of lip-synched mania. I'm crazy for all of this — you,
the kids, the work, the words — and I can
pack it all away before the next student
arrives for their appointment.

On the drive home, silhouettes of tin boats are cut out
of the lake's refracted light and time is a lyric
repeated, is those imagined old guys, their trucks
and trailers left on the side of the highway.

Days loll beneath them, slap against the side
of the boat as I pass, glance in the rear-view mirror
to make sure I've remembered the milk
packed in ice, poems written in hopes that it keeps.

Play Off Season

The boy bobbed in and out of the ditch,
played chicken with the highway,
so light and quick I thought he was
a plastic bag blown full of wind.

Every time I drive past the place
where I stopped and coaxed
the four-year-old to safety, I calculate
averages, chances, the years it will take
to write children, raise books, whatever.

I've been told that my family is complete
— no need then to crouch by the side
of the school and flick hockey cards, trying
to get one last one — a Lemieux, a Gretzky —

though the great ones I aspire to aren't
boys or girls but pages, each book
an unborn child, each child an unwritten book.
Obviously, that's not how it works —

the world even more than hope, my kids
the odds, my books the things that might happen
between strain and luck and dishwater.

A mid-career player, I've learned
that a broken nose can be reset,
teeth spit out, replaced. There are things
no one can take yet my greed

still exceeds my time, my talent. I want
more. Messy, fractured, worn —
more. I want to forget that I can skate
only forward, knock-kneed, not back,
that I can't drink from the kind of cup
I want.

Frame

No way am I going scurry across
the rock face that rises from this lake
like you do so I'll wade around it,
though I know my bones will ache clear
through my skin in the water.

It will be good, you've promised me
— the carcass and rotting meat
of an elk that must have fallen
before the first snow, preserved
until the thaw. I'll like it,

you say, the way it disembodies
time, impermanence, how the cold
can stop and start the process,
freeze-frame the body between,
make winter timeless.

You drop into the deepest baritone,
a sketchy accent, and tell me
that you will take the very finest bone,
clean and dry and pointed, and press it
against the wet arch of my foot

until beads of blood appear
like small berries in spring —
then we laugh and joke about Christ
and disciples, poetry and bloodletting.
But we're too cold or not clever enough,

the elk isn't where you remembered it
and there is a rock face to climb
or water to wade through again before
we can figure out which jokes work,
what stanzas might form.

The elk watches us through the trees,
doesn't move until we leave, then shakes
off the last snow, lifts its hooves high
over deadfall, and moves inland.

Joanna Smythe
Prince George

᧐

translations of the rain

she has a deer's heart
killed by the farmer turned logger
who escaped to Port Clements

she'll send it home to her father
though it is her own heart in truth —
she recognizes the wilderness within
as yet unpopulated

      soft growth coats the graves at Masset
      where she writes in green graffiti
      with bones coughed up by the moss

      her breath caught in a stagnant moment
      moist lips and licking tongue
      mumble translations of the rain

      epitaphs
      especially the homemade one in concrete
      formed from an aluminum roasting pan

      a small mound lies divided from the others
      by a fence
      not a pet but a baby
      lost before baptism

she will always stand outside the fence
it never held her anyway,

caught in the rhythm of her own feet
eyes cast down in a search for words
she is hypnotized by the stones on the beach
her mouth fills with sounds of surf

she is poised on the curve of a wave,
the point of indecision

      she bends low
      long white hair tumbles in the grass —
      surfaces with a clutch of chanterelles
      sixty years ago
      she wrote a report on the Haida Indians
      this schoolgirl from across the Atlantic
      as far away as one can go

heart in the cooler
she will travel home
              sometime
with her offering that tastes
of the embrace
of strangers

this northern lake

I
the bird observed
by the eyeless gaze of sky
is surveyed
and endlessly reflected

between the silvered rhythms
and wash of open water
its wings cut through air
in thrusts
mirrored by delicate fins
on torpedoed bodies
beneath

this northern lake

II
clouds bulk
over Teapot Mountain
its cold stare carried below
the surface   the Summit

a boat is held between
air inside   water out

III
the lake   a lens
its edges fringed
with spruce and balsam
an aperture enclosing
at once a barrier
and intersection
of light

its thin skin sells
the sky
back to itself
in perpetual admiration

arctophobia

inhabits the margins —
the liminal edges of civilization
and its counterpoint of wild space

      a cold black hole that shunts fear
      into the moment where legs won't move
      and words won't do

there is nothing to say to the lake anyway
it deflects sound and meaning
language breaks apart
letters tumble and float away

      the dog knows how to chase
      where to nip
      and growl —
      defends his territory

a limbic translation
equals motion

disconnects this primordial
encounter of fear
and memory

Carly Stewart

Prince George

deterring our minds some

place further than necessary
what we do is not who we are,
but the water keeps lapping up to our armpits
my father says that the snow reached to there & somehow that's appealing

when i speak through a headset w/ love

silence simultaneous
swedish, french, arabic floats heavy over the glass-encased room,
dogs & flip-flops outside the door;
a man with a glass eye & a long fingernail wants 65 baht
for my interactive stay.

sand rifles between toes & the filter of white transposes
my nauseated figure; sarong
heavy [b(r)each] recompense for shadows of past
up to my waist in saltwater,
nipped three times in one day by crabs;
i reach forgiveness. it appears on my fingers

when brain coiled coral can't eradicate the ice that's still in me
meant to snap a photo   hands without mittens
scraping frost off a windshield;
the heat pours over   unwelcomed cup a' tea,
no complaint for winter.   ginger floats loose, i nurse another
people keep flowing, flooding   tide
at sunrise brings no upset,
we deter our minds sometimes
with movies   &   mescaline   &   parrotfish

[kissing on the beach = sand grinding between teeth]

frothing on a sea of discontent,
i reach the sardines flapping w/ fins, no arrows
only to scream inside a snorkel   [my friends' laughs lapping up a tan]
a wall that moves too slowly   their eyes blinking innocence:
shark retired for the day. that can't be undone,

a german soap opera star meditates to house music, says
there is anger   there
illiterate fans enjoy long sexist poetry grinding against stereo
types cover the prattling of mediocre minds
to find real meaning   there behind

a rubbish bin, a concrete plank
where the sewage passes   next to a bar
beach where fire keeps spinning;
the western body transposes   (me]at)market
onto men who need white babies,
a ticket   to coolum where she parades her own fashions &   wishes
(for the guests to stay longer in her b&b)   he won't come home.

the yogis say that tantra's the answer,
a perfect   ;   to the disease that ails
those who *die of thirst on the shore of a lake*

those who *drown on the shore of a lake.*

full shot to skeletons

is nothing like (loving)   full stop,

short stop power lines cut the sky; sparse ponderosa frame the centre
golf and curling, "where's your bikini?" the troll asks the snack shack girl
young enough to be his daughter,
[they study the same] charred pine acts out the trees
pose: arms folded, across a table she chokes

i tried my best to leave this all on your machine
                                                                time
lapse to airbrushed belly,   a soundtrack for hunger
peel back, inside out and gorging on peanut butter mid-sleep
walk the plank,   hip sway — protruding pelvis
he shakes her shoulders,   *mirror images* shower from his grip
peeling carrots, her flesh flakes
[it clings to the bone] is satiated by (k[N]eeding)
dough. fold, sprinkle flour, stir jam, down vodka,
recipes afford another lullaby   *everything looks perfect from far away*

hollywood hoarding ells of skeletons,   trophies of success
while the lineup at the drive-thru grows incessant
drama queens and movie screens none   too lean
scales and reflections break — lie up a sugar bowl mountain
cobra pose in a basin of glacial throw up and we've got two for the road.
his eyes pose questions, he turns his back to [hear her] answer
sequence shots narrow the arrival of her shell, loose to taut
black-smeared lids blink back.

shoot smaller frame to impossible size   smoking
cleaning, living perfection. her friends are silent   in fashion magazines,
(fleece downed women with real flesh are full of back talk)
mouths open in ecstasy, "agency" in submission   coke coated
nostrils wiped away with wet panties   the man with the lens snaps
            [he] will see us waiting from such great heights

measurements of hurt (full, half) feed themselves down (up) throats
cracks: the branch that holds the noose, it's raining cardboard   cut-outs
ice grovels over body, white blanket relief, the synapses stop

                              puzzle pieces from the grave

Si Transken

Prince George

ა

Sunday Shift

pink-cheeked & gentle i've walked to work on this mellow
roots-swelling buds-bursting spring morning. reading
notes, signs, scents & sounds in the air

i prepare to do room checks.

always i scan the phone room, smoke room, group areas, washrooms,
the kitchen, gauging what might be found or hidden behind
their not-private bedroom doors.

i learned quickly

that here kitchen surfaces really are Rorschach assessment tools.
if there's food on the floor, the counters are clumpy & crumbed —
if there are spill-sticky spots, dirty dishes piled,

burn on the stove's dark spirals, grease on the whites of its centre

i can anticipate sour moods, anger, a cranky waking up.
when i knock on & unlock their doors i am sensitive
& still feel somehow responsible when

they hurt, crack or alcohol binge, damage themselves, disappear.

this particular morning three women greet me smiling easily
(like three senior Persian cats in the sun). quietly, they're sharing
recipes & advice about bread making. three fresh loaves

proudly stand there on the counter.
white flags of truce & warm smell of victory over
another dark night, temptations into regression, urges to punish each other

urges to accept punishment for things they've never done,
never done to each other but which have been done
to them somewhere, by someone.

now they're spreading calm ambiguity, an unexpected acceptance,

butter, jam on loaves they've created themselves for each other
& the others. all this affirming human tenacity. all this
possibility for recovery & discovery they share with me.

Distinguish This

what can be said to distinguish this
dirty bowl geography & epistemology —
this unsure & wobbly 50/50 place?

a place where the tracks/roads/rivers cross
& head away with some other purpose perhaps
not of the making of those here now

thousands of years of First Nations trading here,
ninety years of settlement
& unsettlement

& then a university changed the landscape from
its too-cliché-to-say perch up on the greenest spot
with the slippery hill going up & down

teaching & learning changed some dynamics;
other power-flows remained the same but
differently textured & differently trapped in text

some say that university's got the million dollar med program
for 20 students & no bus shelter for the hundreds
who catch the bus in bitter seasons

no one speaks into the microphone to say
the campus may be a puppet or research slave
for corporate etcetera donators

no one *says* the company
gives scholarships, gifts, handshakes
like politicians for their own purposes & pleasures

academia's management is
drawn from those ranks & others are young
& belligerently optimistic

the art gallery of our new millennium
draws letters of complaint
when it asks city council for funding
& slightly more letters of affirmation —

the surpise is as much that newspapers printed
supporters' letters instead of homophobic rants

half the population is newcomer
with boxes unpacked, half are waiting
for that job ad, that change, that chance elsewhere
the halves are always mixing
half-empty half-full half holding the bag
half not wanting to add it all up

everyone knows or is someone who tree-plants,
tree-kills, tree-processes,
everyone knows or is someone

with asthma or other ailments from the pulp mill
there's not much that can be changed
but lots of people are shortchanged

everyone's life is linked to First Nations ways
& means & some are mean about it
& some wholesomely aren't

in January a warning was issued that someone
was stealing purebred boxers, the news is filled
with complaints about biting dogs

hoards of stray Siamese here & hundreds of
companion animals are euthanized each year
cuz people don't plan far in advance or use a vet

buses don't run on Sunday but as of last year
they run as late as 10:00 on a Saturday
& drivers welcome you by first name

meanwhile, every year there are more & more options
for buses, trains, planes *leaving* — & those drivers
don't want to know

Bullies with Designer Lipstick

icing-sugared suburban good white girls have so much
to let go of in my courses &, of course, why should they?

they've come to the profession seeking voyeuristic pleasure, status,
affirmation of all they feel they already know about
bad women who make bad choices, do bad things
with bad men or bad substances.

admitting their made-lovely implications & collusions would
take room away from their pedestal, their ability to direct
their fine noses toward the sunshine their
gracious God has shone on them.

recognizing their contingency in a malestream world
(where big daddies, big brothers, big banks
know best & are taking care of *their* girls' best interests)
would mean they might have to feel

feel how the bottoms of *their* feet are standing
on someone else's shorn down opportunities
when i tell them to get empathetic, to take the bus, live in a shack,
care for so many children that they don't know what to do

they think of nursery rhymes and coloring books
or re-wallpapering their dining room.
they think of just buying new books. they think of
throwing the book at me, complaining to the dean, the judge, the boss.

they think of sin that shouldn't have been indulged in.
they've been pampered into believing that
their Father who art in heaven & the stockbrokers art of *their* fathers
& forefathers who are on the two-car garage side of town

have earned, built, harvested all things fairly.
i am the witch, they think, who babbles, who comes to class unprepared,
isn't professional, has anger management problems,
must be a lesbian (and thus inevitably, infinitely, sour)

just doesn't know how to treat them with the respect
& deference they know they've bought, bought into & bet on.
& having risen to here from the ranks of dirty bad girls i predict
these students are Right & will have their heritage & investments rewarded.

compounded.

Purple

for Dahne Harding & Carl Jung

what happens when blue & red get mashed.
a color not associated with any holiday.

a lovely old-fashioned lamp mysteriously placed
in the modern restaurant i'm writing this in.

the odd color of some people's gums,
grape Kool-aid, popsicles, gumballs,

ostentatious plumage on exotic birds or
in bruises, welts, wounds.

the color of penises in rape & oral assault
stories told to me or written by victims.

are there hundred-dollar bills this color?
thousand-dollar bills this color?

velvety petunias in my gram's garden in the years
before she became too ill to care strongly.

deep purple rock music. deep purple feeling when stoned.
deep purple as a fantasy place i never found.

excessive, extravagant hue that belonged to kings
& religious leaders, now stolen back by us.

meat slabs, veined with white & red, on an old freezer
thawing in the second restaurant job i quit.

only ever had one outfit this color:
a Danskin disco waitress outfit i wore &

sweated in when i was a 110-pound 18-year old:
it made the tips of my tits stand up & it made me tips.

a word i thought i had no thoughts about
but, as so often happens, i was wrong.

Casual Pleasures of Aging Well

Two of the three buildings in which the sexual abuses occurred
are gone now. one burned years ago,
the second recently got ripped down
& replaced by a massive modern structure.
the third exists for different purposes.

all the squares of dirt are owned by different hands.

not forgiving. not forgetting. acknowledging
& monitoring through distance in detachment.

no one did or would talk.

reports to Children's Aid went nowhere.
and all this was before the invention of cyberporn
or i might have had hard evidence,
collaborating testimony from co-victims.

it's hard to be certain of the numbers.
it depends on where you set your perimeters.
but two of the worst are dead: one of a heart attack,
one eaten by cancer. maybe more have died.
i know one is in the clutches of chronic illness.

i can't know everything. my life is too full
of joy, learning, educating, going forward.

Protest Prep 101

before you leave for the gig pay vivid attention to
the weather's potential moodiness.
summer protests don't demand as much outfitting or forearming:
sunglasses, skin protection, maybe an umbrella if the universe
all above you isn't silvery blue.
a coffee cup that can be closed with a handle that
can hook onto something you're wearing
or slide easily into your backpack
(and is hard enough to use as a weapon?).
bring water too.
Kleenex to blow your nose or wipe your tears.
Halls to keep your throat clear might be important.
have on you: a powered-up cellphone, headache meds,
a purse mirror, lip gloss & eyeliner (in case you want
to look brightly smart in that "unexpected" news photo
or police photographs taken from afar).
wear ID in case you're arrested or run over.
carry all your prescription pills: you can't be sure when you'll make it home.
portable protein, like almonds, can assist you
well into the darkest moment & you'll only have to
dust the salt off your gloves.
protests in September require layering, gloves
(not mitts cuz you've got to hold signs & eat almonds).
if this event is happening in mean winter
bring extra socks & a zip-lock bag to stash your wet
ones (there's always a public bathroom somewhere
or a car you can change in).
layer scarves, sweaters, dreams, beliefs. wear earmuffs.
bring enough money to buy coffee & a snack
in case nothing has been provided by the organizers.
be an organizer. befriend organizers. remember the hoards
of organizers who've made your century & your life better.
carry a pen & paper to capture new comrade's contact info.
optimistically give out your own.
most importantly: try & prepare
lots of funky quotes, stories, quirky jokes,
cuz your comrades need that uplift & if they're
robust radical angels, they're prepared as well for their time — maybe long,
long times — of keeping you company, too.

Dancing at Another Feminist Party

my gram's moved on but her melancholy patience
made it possible & probable for me to have carefree moments.

Emma Goldman ain't here but her stamina, charisma
& glorious chutzpah are.

grade school teachers who lent books, enlivened urges,
directed quests — they're not here but their-my-our
best appetites to learn are.

Carol Adams is making vegan meals far away.
Jane Adams made her mark & left us — but her tenacity, audacity,
certainty that we'd find righteous equality are here.

friends we had & stood by for an era, a time, a task
in schools, pool halls, jobs, neighbourhoods —
buddies who helped us laugh & continue — some aren't here
to tell us yet more truth we need to hear
but our sense of humour & ordinary honour are.

Jane Rule, Adrienne Rich, Marge Piercy
are fiercely invoking delicious trouble somewhere today.

Bell Hooks is busy writing books.

Lee Maracle & Lee Lakeman aren't with us tonight
but their calls for anti-racism, organic wisdom, everyone's
sovereign freedom are.

Margrit Eichler, Sandra Acker, Roxana Ng
are in Toronto smartly disturbing people greatly & ruining
patriarchal worlds one lesson at a time.

not every woman who lived & died in process
of pressing forward, addressing unkindness, messing up
Man's efforts to suppress, oppress, & depress us — not every
bold & emboldening woman is in this room
right now expressing sparkly red solidarity

but we are.

Patricia June Vickers

Terrace/Victoria

∽

Peradventure

I was born from the Sodom & Gomorrah
Of my country's greed
The burning accumulation
Of my country's greed
The consummated degradation
Of my country's greed

I was nursed on the salt breast of Lot's wife
Of my people's suffering
Suckled on the nipple of agony
Of my people's suffering
Gazed into the salty hollow eyes
Of my people's suffering

I was raised in the fire of destruction
With my ancestor's blood on my hands and my feet
Breathed the smoke of corruption, devastation and deception
With my ancestor's blood on my hands and my feet
Cried in the corners of the nation's darkness
With my ancestor's blood on my hands and my feet

I was raped then married to colonial oppression
Split in two by the principles of hatred
Bore the offspring of victimhood
Split in two by the principles of hatred
Fed the household of internalized injustice
Split in two by the principles of my country's hatred

In my broken, raging, twisted, damned emptiness
My exile to the margins of your unconsciousness
My imprisonment to your broad ignorance
My enslavement to your single-eyed bigotry

My alienation to your kindness
I fell down to the   bottom
Abraham's angels found me

I was born from the northwest coast
Where gale force winds whipped tree-long canoes on crests of thunder
Where mariners wore cedar-bark hats
Where mile-high waves searched sea-traveller's souls
Where sun-scorched brown-skins met reflections of courage
Journeying to distances unknown

I was nursed on the breast of tenderness
On sweet milk from berries picked
Caressed with the soft worn hands of root diggers, bark peelers, medicine makers
Rocked to the songs of stillness, quietness, gentleness
Carried near the beating, pounding heart of courage
Lovingly wrapped on the back of the women

I was raised by the heart of the hunter
Whose eyes could bring down a seal, sea lion, deer, goose
Near the shovel of a clam digger, canoe carver, masked dancer
By the hand of the halibut hook, fishnet, fish-trap maker
To the drumbeat of the nox-nox dancer
In safety led by the steps of the warrior men

I am married to the principles of the Ayaawx[1]
I bore the children from lineage that stretches to the morning star
I feed the household of warriors of peace, wisdom weavers, soul retrievers, creation speakers
I keep the fire in the house of the ancients
Eat at the table with the family born from raven's light
Rest in the village on the northwest coast

[1] Ts'msyen Ancestral Law.

Swanaskxw

The cedar trees have burned to the ground
There are no grave boxes to hold the corpse
only the stench of smoldering charcoal
Blow westerly wind
lift this weighted sorrow
wipe tear-rimmed downcast eyes
breathe into what remains Naxnox of Sacred Heart
Ascend from vapor and ash
Oh Thunderbird
spread your wings to the corners
scream out with ember eyes
sing skyward
liimk of
halaaytm swanaskxw[2]

[2] Song of healer (the one who heals with the breath). The Naxnox are the supernatural beings that reside in specific geographic areas of the Ts'msyen, Nisga'a and Gitxsan people.

Northwesterly Naxnox

The wind changed
northwesterly Naxnox won the fight
She clenched her covering
turned her face inward
and listened to her ancestors pull

A steady enduring rhythm pierced Ocean's surface

Scar tissue marked her forehead
skin healed from the cut of deception
The cedar vessel buoyed her quest for immunity
Emptied by her love's absence despair is her wake
from twisted bedsheets the child lay in hushed silence

A steady enduring rhythm pierced Ocean's surface

Surrounded by darkness
fear revisited through a crack in the mind's door
North wind Naxnox was merciless
Her hair blew unfurled by cold fingertips
crouched with knees to support fallen thought

A steady enduring rhythm pierced Ocean's surface

Her prayer evoked starlight
The moon will emerge from behind the cloud
A steady enduring rhythm will find her heart
pierce an ocean of desolation
restore childhood moments of delight
sing worn thoughts to silence

She bends

Straddled on longhouse peak
Stone-split cedar shakes sag below my feet
depressions and separations, decay and rot
No sure footing
paused near roof's edge uncertainty teeters
on the precipice of darkness
From a whispered prayer her form emerges from the periphery
her branched arms embrace fear with song
Cradled in Red Alder's aroma that cures our salmon
she bends to place earth below my feet

Separation

Your thoughts accustomed to solitary outcomes
my mind tangled in the barbed wire
bleeds stale madder of want
Your head turns away
my mind flails ragged and torn
screams the pitched cry of a tortured hare thrashing for freedom
Your eye shuts the door
my mind quakes with desperation

Insidious helplessness in adult shape

Languid prayer pulse summons magic
Breath of Naxnox sketches wings
with single lucid movement
release of want sanctions flight

Denielle Wiebe

Prince George

when we are twenty-four again tomorrow

and will we then wear dark sunglasses in broken-down morning cars | i mean when the
ones we love are done with us | when former lovers buy easy flowers for legitimate
spouses | when boys and girls that used to flail their arms and converse loudly in
loud crowded bars get excited about improvements in leak guard and recite the
colour consistency and pitch of a family flu epidemic | will we plunge our dishevelled
heads into americanos and wait for the afternoon to grow dandelions crabgrass and
acetaminophen | if they teethe on hardwood floors in beige houses next to grey houses
next to tidy asphalt driveways a god's-eye view or a crow's-eye view will look very
much like a barcode | but there should always be second-story apartments where
houseplants are named after balding fictional characters and suicidal poets | lined up
with the cigarette butts on the patio we might tilt our heads and perplex our eyebrows
at the absurdity of red red flowers | blooming from the wrists of wilted lovers who
write passionate letters in beige and hide them under posturepedic mattresses

under the philosophers' stones

in a black zip hoodie
peppermint trumps bubble gum & takes the next
ferris wheel to heaven.
           (i hear you clucking your tongue from
              way up there in your poet-tree)

angel in the sand & satan
in snowshoes. hand in hand,
right there under your arm.   shruggin' off a river.
                      shruggin' into a photograph
of girls in bikinis & blue satin sashes
swaying their asses & batting eyelashes

at all the philosophers
sitting around & scratching their stones,
peeking up the virgin's robe
at the ascension,   where they spy

walmart shoppers & those
control top pantyhose fading into phosphorescent

legs & nuclear arms shrugging into cardigan sweaters
(i'd shrug, but you've got the shoulders).

older & older we'll resort to cellophane and roses
resigned & redesigned (we sigh:

none of the gynoholics in the penis club
                are ever gonna menstruate).

cash in on chronic fatigue & congestive heart failure.
stash orchids in orgasms
       in photo safe scrapbooks
       full of bubble gum, pantyhose, & poetry.

wet siren

that saturday night in bombay, when i found my spine
i accidentally swallowed it.

so, *red,*
    i said   more like a siren than a wet wagon, really.

(later that night, a backache
& a bitter taste   running
                 from my mouth).

nightmares lit with street lights. a truck
in the university parking lot, loaded
with empty beer cans & the leftover skeleton
of a christmas tree.

a cigarette is such a long time to sit still.
yes, love is a truck with no windows.

shoes in the doorway.
& feet dancing in fresh green sheets.
                (this guy wakes me up
             to tell me i was crying in my sleep).

well, some of these bad dreams are soft like milk
& vanilla.   & all those stars
             were such a big mistake.

in the morning, head hanging
over soft vertebrae, a cigarette is still such a long time
to sit in all this sunlight

& those mean things i said to you. those nice things
i said to be mean.

nursery rhyme

static is the sound of sudden downpour
in a house made of plastic wrap.

i oughta be sneaking
kisses under
these 12" hanging baskets.
   spontaneous rain. the sky is
   lit with electric webs.
   smell: barely ventilated
       cucumber blossoms
   next to tomato stalks.

no, i'm not the sun
& i'm not
a pepper plant.
    i'm not heat
    or spice.

    but right now i've got rhododendron rain-sounds
    that splash & fade
       like sun-spun crates.

when the seed-house
is swelling   with germination,
    no lyrics grow in my head.

up in the retail greenhouse,
elderly ladies mill about.
white runners step
stepping thru aisles, towing
black wagon wheels.

silhouettes thru saran-glass.

a simple trout

love is the dumbest thing
to write about. the word itself
is a kid with a minnow net. the concept
is what i want him
to catch.

so the kid, he brings me a net full of minnows,
rocks, weeds, & algae. & what the fuck
am i supposed to think, except
i got it all
wrong.

or maybe this
is really it, but all i want
is a simple trout. or better
yet, a trout's heart caught in a net.

but even hearts are full
of other stuff & blood, and what
do fish & their hearts have to do

with love, or why
is the kid a boy, & is the net
supposed to be part of it or not?

too bad the kid didn't catch me
a trout, & i didn't give him a heart,
& all i've got is a mixed net full of love scraped
from the bottom of a lake & crusted
with algae & smelling of fish, & the real
problem here — what i'm trying to get across —
is i'm not even sure i like kids
as much as metaphors

Gillian Wigmore
Prince George

gaps in the downtown revitalization efforts, september two thousand eight

pg leaves its burn victims out to air in the foetid fall inversion that traps the pulp mill fumes in the river bottom where the bulk of the downtown falls to the arsonist, historic building by building, the free press out to catch it as it tumbles

aspen leaves float yellow down from the treetops, the yearly striptease in the parks, the catcalls of the wind, the sidewalks so deep in detritus it's hard to know where to walk, a pretty contrast between leafen gold and blackened wood

downtown you might be accosted for money or to buy drugs, where the man who offers crystal meth says sorry like a gentleman when he sees the baby in the pack on my back, says didn't see the little bugger, dreadfully sorry, ma'am

so ask: does the cost outweigh the benefit of ripping a half-burned building down? we could do it with our teeth but when the rafters are exposed will the homeless teem out like rats or secrets and we'll feel ashamed we sleep warm at night?

nights we don't go out, might see a woman who looks too much like me offering her goods too cheap on george street. the kids say why's it called queensway and I imagine that: the queen on a tour of the prince george downtown

the burned-out buildings are a calling card of the heart's, the singed hulls of old hotels too vivid a picture of the actual town we outlie in the suburbs, living sweetly though our eyes burn in the fall from the pulp mill fumes and all that acrid smoke

Pine: a love story

the lodgepole   *the ponderosa*

hello

he breaks off a husk of vanilla
      bark from the breast of a giant:
a gift of ponderosa —

           how do you do?

encroaching

crowds of pine
where one would do

a tree needs space
to   stretch   out

          fronds
            and branches

hers

pine flats, spruce bogs
those dark spicy forests
of home, thigh-deep in tree litter
midday scent of dry needles baking in the duff

and his

bare hillsides   sentinels

      sweetness in air

neither is easy with how it's turned out

epidemic of richness —
too many pine
packed in each against his brother
a frenzy
              of sway   and reach

slow epidemic of beautiful death —
a palette of new colours:
                        red, scarlet, grey, black, rust
        the still dark heart
        crusted sloughed bark

                  clear-cut

double high trucks — a northern interlude

blue rings on pecker poles
        trees so thin
        stacked so many deep

the claimed imperative of logging: we must
because we don't know
what would happen if we didn't

afraid of: the standing water at the base of the trees
           the threat of fire

watching from a pickup truck made small
by the sight of the overloaded
                  rounding a hairpin

on a sunday road
(they log through the weekend
don't bother to hide the scree from the highway)

we see at the centre of the attack zone:

no beetles
the pretty blue aftermath
the richest seasons of hauling in years
the sepia tone to the photos
age and smoke creeping in on the edges
the whiff of toppling throughout the spending spree
we are wide-eyed
and small
weak-voiced in this time of must-do and action

Okanagan early summer

free baby trees at the dominion day celebrations,
heat like a curse —
beyond the lake the dry hills are furred with pine.
people brush sweaty arms in passing,
wear dark glasses to block out the light and the populace.
they cleave together, a copse, an experimental forest,
paired and procreating,
each bending with the others' wind,
moving so the light reaches the little ones,
their roots shallow
their crowns so desperately heavy.

two types of pine

not the real thing, but the memory —
the rush of air through long needles
susurrus of wind through high bald branches
after it and also
the rough itch of a scab, the lying tang of healing
after massacre and amputation ...
what after massacre and amputation?

every love happens on the cusp of some apocalypse

vanilla and spice

culmination of weather and hatch
the cash in the boom
the fall

standing, despite the onslaught,
where great beasts timbered,
making beams with the alaskan mill.
working side by each, sawdust in the work gloves,

everything pale green and new

bather at a spring

before the school group comes around the bend
and startles the birds from the beech trees
before the clouds bunch and gather in front of the sun
before the rain slicks the paths impassable
just this: a spring rimmed with astelia
and the naked length of a man

his gaze down, the great bulk
and meat of him, tawny
muscled, the mountain air
pinking the tips of his nipples
the dark hair standing stiff

when he reaches for the water with one foot
his toes extend in advance of the shock
there is no record of a shriek
or a leap from the water, no scrambling
onshore, no shimmying wet
into salt-thick clothes

just this: a moment, a spring
crowded in with beech and sword fern
a forest, a man
and every great or tiny thing
that comes after, packed
into the taught purse of his skin
his naked thigh
his held breath

Debbie: two things:

I've got to go about collecting the women because we lie where we're strewn
due to weather, childbirth, patterns of the wind, hopelessness, depression
drugs prescribed before other avenues are pursued
here I am perusing the alleys and lanes
here is Prince George on a map
I don't have a cellphone or a GPS — I'm waiting for a sign
from Demeter or her daughter

*

dear Debbie,
if we make a deal
that hurdles all obvious means
of communication and connection
just through foresight (the wile required
to overcome the phobias of phone and mail)
how does that equate to greater return
on creative outputs?
it does, doesn't it?
I'm writing, aren't I?

*

the women here man the counters and crosswalks
they fill the coffee cups and direct traffic
a woman delivered your mail
a woman delivered your child
I see them at the mall and on the street
I wave even if they loiter on Queensway
I'm writing my way toward them
a woman writes for the radio
she talks in your ear
but it's a whisper since nobody's listening

*

I find you on the soccer pitch and our eyes connect
I know your birth stories without your confession
I was in the corner near the foetal heart monitor
I watched her crown
or was that me? when you watched me
or when we traded stories like artist's trading cards

190

frayed at the edge, deliberately miss-sewn
and at the end you come out a humble survivor
when really you/we are the heroine(s)

*

where are the women writing in PG?
here   more secret than you'd anticipate
I hear a woman on the radio driving the ice road
another sister speaking for the executive of the union local
we're writing in the air
for the audience in the sky
our children take dictation
when they pause mid-step to listen

*

playground dust clogs my throat, pleasantries
stick   I won't pretend they don't
Marian drove a tank of gas to fumes
ferrying her brood from the Hart to the pool to the school and back home
her husband drives a Bronco
I only wrote that because
I want to drive a Bronco

*

dear Debbie
my daughter's learned to read and when she reads she reads
for sustenance — I feed her books with women heroes
but she asks for Astro Boy and Smurfs
Debbie, where are the women writing?
and why does the playground scare me?
I ask only
because you look as shocked as I
to be a feminist
hard at work house-wifing
hard at work house-minding
hard at work wondering   just what the fuck happened
to land a girl like me   here
in the hinterlands
settling for what our foremothers
bucked so hard against?

*

they read the sides of cereal packets
they read the back of the toothpaste squeeze tube
they read the stalls of the park's public toilet
tag by tag, each cuss word a spark across the retina

*

Debbie
I found your long poem
like a letter I'd neglected to answer
so: hello? hello?
I had this phobia
but I'm over it

spring

the hawks are out hunting mice in grass past gold,
now brown, dry and dead. the hawks, humourless,
hunt, merciless and I miss you, done with waiting —
the mice cowering, then shitting paths scooting past
trying to get something to eat, getting et instead — I miss you,
I said. water in the fields and raptor's wide arcs,
circles, patience — shadows inscribing the water
so the ducks and scoters scatter on the creek bulge,
take to air awkward, half-winged, scurry and regroup.
redtails and kestrels on the power lines glare at the grass,
the steely water, the cows hock-deep in melt-off — I
miss you — waiting for the strike, for feathers to fall. hunting
or watching — wanting only to eat or be fed, birds staring
ground-ward, me staring skyward: seeping or bleeding out,
wary, all the same.

Alice Williams
Damdochax Lake

∽

Intemperate Rainforest

Trees on the ridgeline
bending in half;
at a hundred-feet tall, not to
be taken lightly.

When the wind hit the water,
it was a flattened sheet
of silver metal,
sent the canoes on the dock skyward
then lost down the lake in high waves.

Trees floated thru the air
standing upright, broken off
at thirty feet, the wind carrying them
'til they crashed all over.

Only the birches held their ground
their powerful gnarly roots clinging
deep in the earth, bending but not breaking
as the others, spruce and balsam.

Then the rains came,
up one side of the valley
and down the other;
a solid driving waterfall;

after that, the sky full of light
pink and orange and baby blue
swirling and changing,
giant clouds whirling
a cosmic blend
calming,
then slowly
becoming still.

Tom

Moving loads with the
helicopter,
straight down
two hundred feet.
Netloads, slingloads
longlines, lumber.
High-speed and loud,
wound up.
The pilot
large and slow,
counterpart
to his machine.
So calm,
an artist in the air.

Waiting for the Float Plane

An echo in the wind,
that first faint note
a vibration in the air
not noise yet,
but a feeling
that fills the body.

Poetry

I'm in the wind,
bigger now —
clear water
over stones.

Black specks fall from the sky
impossibly tiny.
A day later,
movement.
Later still,
infant caterpillars.

Her leaving was a sudden hurtful blow
even if I was ready for it.

Wild rocks
shaped by the river
art objects, tools, letters;
we bring them home
to use as touchstones.

I found a hundred
heart-shaped rocks.

Put them in the foundation
of our new building.

Contributors

After years of travelling, **Jacqueline Baldwin**, born and educated in New Zealand, raised her three children as a single parent on her organic farm beside a wildly beautiful river in the Canadian Rockies. She has performed over four hundred public readings and won ten literary awards. Her book, *Threadbare Like Lace,* on the BC bestseller list in 1998, is now in a sixth printing. She was named by the *Prince George Free Press* as one of the people who "make a difference, shake the status quo, and rattle the bars of conformity." Her biography appears in the *Canadian Who's Who.* She is the designer and facilitator of the workshop *the Healing Art of Story.* Jacqueline now lives in Prince George, in a house surrounded by trees and good neighbours. She feels privileged to be among welcoming people who support creative endeavours and are committed to building and maintaining strong community.

Leslie Barnwell was born in Victoria. She came to Kispiox Village in 1975 to teach grade two and has remained in the beautiful Kispiox Valley ever since. Her written work has been published in several magazines including *Northword, Confluence* and *Geez* (she won the *Geez* writing contest in 2008 and 2009). She is included on the website Poets Against the War and in the anthology *Creekstones: Words and Images,* by Creekstone Press. Creekstone Press also published a book of her poems and drawings entitled *The Rosemary Suite.* She has taught creative writing for the NITEP programme through Northwest Community College and facilitated informal writing workshops in the community. She is also a visual artist (website www.lesliesart.ca) and her poetry is sometimes mingled with that work as well, most recently in an installation piece called *Pond Garden* which was shown in the group show Portals in Terrace, celebrating change in women's lives.

Marilyn Belak was raised in Wynyard, Saskatchewan and Dawson Creek, BC. She has a strong connection to the wilderness, words and birds of the BC Peace Region which she calls home. She is published in Canadian literary journals and chapbooks, is twice featured in Leaf Press' *Monday's Poem* and has read at the Poet's Corner at Word on the Street in Vancouver. In 2008, she collaborated with three women writers to create the "Written in Stone Renga" along Dawson Creek's walking path. Marilyn is a proud alumni of the 2009 Muskwa-Kechika Artists' Wilderness Camp organized by Donna Kane and guided by Wayne Sawchuk. A mother and advocate for the environment, sustainability and social justice, she is a part time Community Care RN and is serving her 8th year on Dawson Creek City Council.

Katherine Bell is a northerner. Born in Kitimat, BC, she spent 13 years away and then returned in 2000 to family, fresh air, rivers and mountains. She now resides at Lakelse, 30 kilometres away from her hometown. She spends a great deal of her time outside: walking through the trails with her dogs and hiking up local mountains where she revitalizes herself. She has been writing poetry for years, but just had a first showing of some of her poetry and photographs as part of the *Portals* Art Show in Terrace, BC in April 2010. Kathy has a Masters degree in Curriculum and teaches Creative Writing and English at a high school in her area.

Growing up in Saskatchewan, **Leanne Boschman** was fortunate to have had poetry read to her, including the ballads of Robert Service. Perhaps the Northern imagery captured her burgeoning imagination. She loved the playful possibilities of rhyme, meter, and imagery. With its expressive, meditative, and devotional potential, poetry is still an important part of her life. Living in Prince George, Terrace and Prince Rupert, she has found the people as well as the landscapes surrounding these Northern communities to be a vital source of inspiration. Her poems have been published in *Other Voices, Dandelion, Room, Geist,* and *Prism International,* as well as several anthologies. *Precipitous Signs: A Rain Journal,* her first volume of poems, was published by Leaf Press in April 2009. At present, Leanne is working on her PhD in the Languages, Cultures, and Literacies program at Simon Fraser University.

Born and raised in Prince George, **Crystal Campbell** returned home to Northern BC after pursuing music studies in Northern Ireland. She rediscovered the joy of writing when she entered UNBC to study English in 2006. While fairy rings left by coffee cups on empty tables are a favorite whimsical muse, Crystal's poetry emerges from the confluence of daily life and the concerns raised by political and academic spheres. Currently completing an MA in English, Crystal is also working on a series of poems entitled *Café Poetica* and a long poem based on her experiences living in Prince George.

Joan Conway moved to Terrace, BC in 1982 because of her deep attraction to northern lifestyles. She settled in the small farming village of Cedarvale where she raised her two sons, grew organic gardens, and worked on her writing and artistic endeavors. For the past ten years she has been employed as a Rehabilitation worker in a Terrace alternative school where she advocates for the rights of youth. Her love for the geography and culture of her home strongly influence her poetry. She has performed readings throughout the northern region. Her work was published in the journals *Connections* and *Northword* as well as *Passages,* published by UNBC. She also wrote the poetry for the documentary, *Spirit of the Raven,* produced by Copycat Video Productions, Terrace.

Barbara Coupé, a professional forester and a mother of two fine young men, has been a Cariboo girl for over 30 years. In 2008, she moved from Williams Lake to Prince George to pursue a Masters in Interdisciplinary Studies at UNBC. Her thesis is a creative nonfiction account of the scientists behind the ecological classification program of the BC Forest Service. She has published poems in the Lillooet-based journal *Lived Experience* and has contributed to Caitlin Press's *Gumption and Grit: Women of the Cariboo Chilcotin*. In 2006, her poetic interpretation of the mountain pine beetle epidemic, "The Ladies Dance," was not only read on CBC Radio and shortlisted for the 2007 Winston Collins/Descant Prize for Best Canadian Poem, but was also translated into the Shuswap language as "Red Clouds Dancing." For Barb, writing poetry lets her play in the sandbox of metaphor and gives her momentum to keep on learning.

Marita Dachsel was born and raised in Williams Lake, BC. After twelve years in Vancouver, during which she received her MFA in Creative Writing at UBC, she now lives in Edmonton with her husband, playwright Kevin Kerr, and their two sons. Her first book of poetry *All Things Said & Done* (Caitlin, 2007) was shortlisted for a ReLit Award. *Eliza Roxcy Snow* (red nettle press, 2009) is a recent chapbook and her poetry has appeared in many Canadian journals as well as part of Vancouver's Poetry In Transit Program. Most of her poems featured in *Unfurled* are part of *Glossolalia*, a manuscript in progress exploring the polygamous wives of Joseph Smith, founder of the LDS Church.

Sarah de Leeuw is a geographer and creative writer as well as an assistant professor with UNBC's Northern Medical Program in the Faculty of Medicine at UBC. She is the author of *Unmarked: Landscapes Along Highway 16* (2004) and her most recent book, *The Geographies of a Lover*, is a collection of poetry forthcoming (2012) with NeWest Press. Her essays "Quick-Quick. Slow. Slow." (2009) and "Columbus Burning" (2008) both won CBC Literary Awards for creative non-fiction. Her poetry has appeared in a number of Canadian literary journals, including *Fiddlehead*, *Wascana*, and *The Claremont Review*. She grew up in Port Clements and Queen Charlotte City (both on Haida Gwaii) and in Terrace.

Pamela den Ouden was born and raised in Montreal. She came to northern B.C. as part of a back-to-the-land movement in the Seventies, living on a communal farm near Pink Mountain on the Alaska Highway. She and her family then settled in Fort St. John, where she still resides. A former writer and editor at a Fort St. John weekly newspaper, she won a national journalism award for a story about the opening of a northern mine. She has worked as a banker, secretary, recruiter, and college English and Women's Studies instructor. She currently teaches English as a Second Language at Northern Lights College.

Fyre Jean Graveline, originally from a Metis bush community in Northern Manitoba, relocated to Prince George in 2008 to work as the Chair of the First Nations Studies program at UNBC. She is a published author of two books, both with Fernwood Press: *Circle Works: Transforming Eurocentric Consciousness* and *Healing Wounded Hearts*. As an artist and Art Therapist, Fyre Jean welcomes all opportunities to educate and heal herself and others through expressive forms, including painting, sculpture, song, poetry and prose. Through the use of Circle and other traditional methods she has well developed skills in speaking from the heart and respectful listening, as well as a sense of humour. She has recently returned home to the East Coast, and through her company www.circleworksconsulting.com is providing advocacy and support services to Indian Residential School Survivors, and is a qualified counselling professional on the Health Canada mental health provider list.

Jamella Hagen grew up in the Bulkley and the Kispiox Valleys near Hazelton, BC. She has a Master of Fine Arts in Creative Writing from UBC and is a former executive editor of *PRISM International*. Her poetry has won the *Fiddlehead's* Ralph Gustafson Prize, placed third in *This Magazine's* Great Canadian Literary Hunt, and appeared in journals and anthologies including *Arc, Event, Room*, and *The Best of Canadian Poetry in English, 2010*. Jamella currently lives in Whitehorse and teaches in the Writing Centre and the School of Access at Yukon College. Her first collection of poetry is forthcoming with Nightwood Editions.

Lisa Haslett (nee deHoog, formerly Close) was born and raised in the Burns Lake area. After many years in other parts of BC, she now calls Prince George home. Lisa is currently completing her Masters degree in English at the University of Northern British Columbia. Her first chapbook *How to Survive the Worst-case Scenario: A Handbook* won the 2008 Barry McKinnon Chapbook Prize.

Jacqueline Hoekstra was born and raised in Northern BC. She grew up on a farm alongside the Skeena River on Braun's Island, just outside of Terrace. Still self-identified with Northern BC, Jacqueline completed and successfully defended her dissertation *Community, culture, nature: Northern BC Women's Ecopoetry* at SFU. Included in her dissertation are poets Donna Kane, Si Transken, Gillian Wigmore, Heather Harris, Dani Pigeau, Sheila Peters, and Joan Conway. Jacqueline lives in Gibsons, BC with her 5 kids, husband, and a variety of animal friends, including dogs, cats, chickens, goats, a pony, and a donkey. She is vice president of The Gibson's Live Poetry Society. Her first published poem was "Old Growth," published by the *Antigonish Review* (1997). She has been published in 3 anthologies, as well as in *Room of One's Own*, and *The Fiddlehead*. "Fishing with my father" is from her chapbook *History Never Repeats* (2007).

Born in California, **K. Darcy Ingram** has lived in BC for 35 years. She recently relocated to Prince George, a region perfect for her hobbies, sensitivities and lifestyle. Favourite things include health care, animals, biking, snowshoeing, and everything found out-of-doors. Darcy graduated in 2007 with a BA in Creative Writing from Vancouver Island University and is starting her MA at UNBC in 2010. BC publication credits include *BackofTheBook, Portal Magazine, Play Ball!, AromaScents Journal,* and *Island Writer Magazine,* while other works were shortlisted in 2010 for both the Barry McKinnon Chapbook Award and the John Harris Fiction Award. Though Darcy writes fiction, features, interviews, non-fiction, prose, and poetry in all forms, her most intense love is performance or Spoken Word poetry (*Portal Magazine* Poetry Slam winner 2005; 2nd place 2006; Survivor Poet for the 2010 Relay for the Cure in Prince George).

Donna Kane lives in Rolla, BC, a few miles northeast of Dawson Creek. Her writing has appeared in journals, magazines and anthologies across Canada. In 2010 she was a winner in the Geist's Literal Literary Postcard Story Contest, and she is the author of two books of poetry, *Somewhere, a Fire* and *Erratic.* In addition to her writing, Donna organizes literary readings, arts festivals, and artist retreats throughout the Peace Liard region. She recently completed a degree in writing at the University of Victoria. She has a website: www.donnakane.com.

Sabrina L'Heureux is a poet who grew up on Vancouver Island. Three years ago, she traded in the rain for snow, and moved north to Dawson Creek. She studied Creative Writing at the University of Victoria, where she also earned a French degree. This summer, she will begin her Creative Writing MFA in the Optional-Residency program at UBC. Her poetry has appeared in *This Side of West,* and on-line at Goblin Fruit, and Utmost Christian Writers.

Caroline Lowther grew up on a farm near Vanderhoof, B.C. Although she has spent most of her life in Vancouver, teaching and raising her children, she still refers to Vanderhoof as home. She enjoys writing poetry because of its ability to evoke emotions, tell a story, or paint a picture. She is grateful for the support and encouragement received from friends and family, especially her mother.

Mary MacDonald has spent the majority of her life in north central British Columbia with time spent away in Victoria, other parts of Canada and Latin America. She grew up in Vanderhoof and has lived in Prince George for over ten years. Her poetry is very much influenced by her political activism on subjects ranging from human rights, health, air and water quality, to economic development in the north. She is one of the founders of two environmental groups in Prince George, People's Action Committee for Healthy Air (PACHA) and Sea to Sands Conservation Alliance. Mary has worked as a lawyer in the past and currently works as a community social worker in health care. She has written for *Northword Magazine* and recently produced a poetry chapbook entitled *The Sparrow's Lament.*

Pua Medeiros has gone through a considerable metamorphosis. When she lived in Kispiox and Prince George, BC and taught in the First Nations Studies Program at the University of Northern British Columbia, she was known as Heather Harris. She moved to Hawai'i to pursue new research interests and married a Hawaiian guy who gave her new names — first (Pua –"Flower") and last. She has since given up the husband but kept the names. Pua now teaches part time at the University of Hawai'i at Hilo, lives in the bush in Nanawale in Puna with her two daughters and goes to Pohoiki (beach) every day. When her (ex-)husband asked her, "Why don't you go home?" she replied, "Because I can go outside every day here." She continues to go outside every day and does not ever, not for one second, miss -40 degrees.

Sheila Peters lives in Driftwood Canyon near Smithers in northwestern BC. Her poetry and fiction has been widely published in Canadian journals. *Tending the Remnant Damage* (Beach Holme 2001) is a linked collection of short stories; *Canyon Creek: A Script* (Creekstone 1998) tells the story of the eviction of a Wet'suwet'en family from its homesite near Smithers. Her most recent book, *the weather from the west*, is a collection of poetry published in collaboration with images by visual artist, Perry Rath. Over the past few years her canoe, Buttercup, has been urging her to get out onto the water more often. She has begun to follow that good advice - exploring the lakes of the upper Skeena watershed and the waters off the northwest coast with the patient guidance of more experienced friends.

Rebekah Rempel grew up in Abbotsford and Tomslake and now lives in Rolla with her husband. She has fourth-year status in the University of Victoria's Writing Department and plans to obtain her BA with a major in poetry. She participated in the *Written in Stone* project that displays a renga in a local park. She has read at several events, including Sweetwater 905, and her work appeared in the Peace-Liard Regional Arts Council's *Arts Beat*. She has hosted two poetry readings in Dawson Creek and hopes to start a reading series in the future to bring more writers to the north. Although she mainly writes poetry, she has also begun writing fiction and a novel, as well as dabbling in photography.

Laisha Rosnau is a poet and novelist who, in her five years in Prince George, created two children and the poetry collection *Lousy Explorers* (Nightwood 2009), which was short-listed for the Pat Lowther Award. Her first collection of poetry, *Notes on Leaving* (Nightwood 2004), won the Acorn-Plantos Award and her novel, *The Sudden Weight of Snow* (McClelland & Stewart 2002), was an honourable mention for the Books in Canada First Novel Award. Laisha is now a resident caretaker of a wild bird sanctuary in Coldstream, BC, with her husband and children. She misses bright, cold winter days in the north.

Joanna Smythe has spent most of her adult life in Prince George and like many Northerners, has a special affinity for the rural and wild areas that are so close and available. Writing has become an interface for her to explore how people make personal meaning through their relationship to the natural world. Her characters manifest themselves from composites of real personalities whose lives inspire observance and response. Recently, Joanna's work has evolved to bring her writing and artwork together in a way that references each other or continues the same narrative. Joanna has put her teaching career on hold to focus on her writing and art practices. She has completed the creative writing component of her Fine Arts Degree at the University of Northern British Columbia. Joanna has been exhibiting her artwork publicly in group shows over the last ten years, but this is her first written publication.

A nomad by nature, **Carly Stewart** will continue to travel this wide earth, leaving her (nearly) invisible footprints wherever she goes. No matter where she is, her narrative self is stamped with all things Prince George, whether they be bleak, beautiful or anywhere in-between. Currently, her manuscript *Ms. Direction*, a collection of short stories about women, mental health, and popular culture, is under consideration at various Canadian publishing houses. She has just finished her Master's in English Literature at UNBC and is teaching English at the College of New Caledonia.

Si Transken was born in northern Ontario and identifies as hodge podge white bush trash being recycled. She has been in northern BC for 10 years and has taught Social Justice oriented courses in Prince George, Fort St. John, Terrace, and Quesnel. Boom/bust economies and settler/First Nations challenges wear on her heart. Resource-based economies often seem to have an allergy to the arts. That pisses her off. Racism, classism, sexism and homophobia piss her off. Nonetheless and all the more necessarily so, she continues to write poetry, do rants for causes, show up for protests, rescue stray cats, and cherish anyone who feeds her steamed vegetables. She has published in *Canadian Women's Studies*, *Atlantis*, and *Capilano Review*, has edited anthologies of creative writing from northern activists, and is blessed to be in a marriage where two poems are poeming.

Patricia June Vickers was born in Prince Rupert in Northern BC. Her father was a fisherman whose own heritage combined three Northwest coast First Nations — Ts'msyen, Haida and Heiltsuk. Her mother was a schoolteacher whose parents had immigrated to Canada from England. Vickers recently completed a Ph.D. at the University of Victoria, her dissertation topic was Ayaawx (Ancestral Law): Transforming suffering. She holds a Bachelor of Education degree and a Master's Degree in Education Psychology. As a published author, Vickers has written extensively on community and mental heath issues as they relate to First Nations' history and ancestral principles. She is also an engaging public speaker with extensive experience developing and delivering presentations and workshops on a variety of topics. Poetry has been a way to carve experience to a single piece of regalia.

Denielle Wiebe was born in Prince George and, while she has moved around a bit, she has spent nearly half of her twenty-eight years there. Her first poems were written for her creative writing classes at UNBC with Rob Budde in 2004, and she has since been published in *The Forestry Diversification Project*, a collection of poems by Prince George writers, and *Norther'*, an online literary publication. Currently she is working on her MA thesis, a project that focuses on the relationships between place and women's development in novels by three of her favourite Canadian writers: Laisha Rosnau, Lisa Grekul and Miriam Toews.

Gillian Wigmore's book, *soft geography*, won the 2008 ReLit award and was nominated for the Dorothy Livesay award. Recently her work was short listed for the *Malahat Review* long poem prize and the Great BC Novel contest. She studied at the University of Victoria and the Banff Centre. Her work has been published in Canadian magazines and anthologized. She was born in Vanderhoof and lives in Prince George, BC.

Alice Williams spent the first four years of her life mainly above timberline west of Babine Lake and Hazelton where her father worked on little mines. She went to school in Smithers and later took creative writing at UBC. For several years she worked as a journalist around the province. In 1978, with her ex-partner, she started Damdochax River Lodge, a fly-in flyfishing camp and wilderness retreat in the upper Nass River watershed, which she still runs today with her daughter. Along with living and working in nature, writing, painting and energy healing are her main passions. www.damdochax.com

About the Cover

Jacqueline Rush Lee

Absolute Depth (From "Ex Libris Series," 1997-2000)
Fired periodical shedding text in water
Installation Detail
H14' x W3.5' x D2

As one who loves books, and the imaginative worlds to which book contents lure their readers, I am drawn to the physicality of the book, as familiar object, medium, and archetypal form.
I am a sculptor who has worked with the book as my primary medium for over twelve years. I transform used books into art works that create new narratives by applying physical and conceptual processes to transform metaphorically. Many of the techniques that I employ are informed by both traditional and non-traditional artistic practices through which I scramble the formal arrangement of the books to create evocative art works that express ideas in veiled layers of meaning.

In 1998 I developed a process to fire books in a kiln without clay slip so that they would be preserved in their pure, transformed state, unmasked by a clay surface additive (*Ex Libris 1998-2000*). Used books were fired in a controlled kiln environment and transformed into fragile, though stable art forms. Once fired the books were no longer recognizable in their usual context, but were transformed into poetic remnants of their former selves, suggesting a trajectory of time, transformation and memory.

Absolute Depth is a fired periodical from the Ex Libris series that is suspended in a tank of water. It was inspired by the point of absolute depth in which a diver could not physically dive deeper into the ocean, as a metaphor for knowledge. Over time, the periodical gently shed its inner text into the water slowly unfurling and creating a new narrative at the bottom of the tank.

Jacqueline Rush Lee is an Anglo-Irish sculptor from Northern Ireland, who lives and works in Kahaluu, on the windward side of Oahu, Hawaii. She has an MFA in Studio Art from the University of Hawaii at Manoa with a BFA in Ceramics with Distinction. Rush Lee has worked with the book as her primary medium for over twelve years. She exhibits her artwork nationally and internationally and her work is in private and public collections. www.jacquelinerushlee.com

Body font: Arno Pro
Named after the Florentine river which runs through the heart of the Italian Renaissance, Arno draws on the warmth and readability of early humanist typefaces of the 15th and 16th centuries.

While inspired by the past, Arno is distinctly contemporary in both appearance and function. Designed by Adobe Principal Designer Robert Slimbach, Arno is a meticulously-crafted face in the tradition of early Venetian and Aldine book typefaces.